The Practitioner Inquiry Series

Marilyn Cochran-Smith and Susan L. Lytle, *SERIES EDITORS*

ADVISORY BOARD: JoBeth Allen, Rebecca Barr, Judy Buchanan, Robert Fecho, Susan Florio-Ruane, Sarah Freedman, Karen Gallas, Andrew Gitlin, Dixie Goswami, Peter Grimmett, Gloria Ladson-Billings, Sarah Michaels, Susan Noffke, Marsha Pincus, Marty Rutherford, Lynne Strieb, Carol Tateishi, Diane Waff, Ken Zeichner

(continued)

Imagination and Literacy

A Teacher's Search for the Heart of Learning

KAREN GALLAS

TEACHERS COLLEGE PRESS

Teachers College, Columbia University
New York and London

The poem that opens Part II, "The House Was Quiet and the World Was Calm," is from *The Collected Poems of Wallace Stevens* by Wallace Stevens, copyright 1954 by Wallace Stevens and renewed 1982 by Holly Stevens. Used by permission of Alfred A. Knopf, a division of Random House, Inc.

Published by Teachers College Press, 1234 Amsterdam Avenue, New York, NY 10027

Library of Congress Cataloging-in-Publication Data

Gallas, Karen.
    Imagination and literacy : a teacher's search for the heart of learning / Karen Gallas.
        p.   cm. — (The practitioner inquiry series)
    Includes bibliographical references and index.
    ISBN 0-8077-4405-0 (pbk. : alk. paper) — ISBN 0-8077-4406-9 (cloth : alk. paper)
        1. Imagination.   2. Creative thinking.   3. Education—Aims and objectives.   I. Title.   II. Series.
    LB1062.G353   2003
    370.15'7—dc21   2003054188

ISBN 0-8077-4405-0   (paper)
ISBN 0-8077-4406-9   (cloth)

Printed on acid-free paper
Manufactured in the United States of America

10   09   08   07   06   05   04   03   8   7   6   5   4   3   2   1

For Alphoniso

Contents

PART II

Building a Literate Identity   59

PART III

Imagination in the Real World   117

Acknowledgments

Heartfelt thanks to the following people: Sarah Huard, my co-teacher in 1995–1996, whose observations from that year were invaluable; members of the Brookline Teacher Research Seminar for their support during the early part of this work; Roberta Herter, who enabled me to gain access to the California State University Library System; Cindy Ballenger, Kelly Demers, Marion MacLean, and Peter Smagorinsky, for their helpful readings of the draft manuscript; Carol Chambers Collins, my editor at Teachers College Press, whose critique so greatly improved this work; my husband, Dave, for his support and encouragement.

And finally, thanks to all the children, beginning with my own two, Liam and Kelsey McNiff, and extending over the years to the many others I have taught. You have helped me grow big with imagination once again.

O Chestnut-tree, great-rooted blossomer,
Are you the leaf, the blossom or the bole?
O body swayed to music, O brightening glance,
How can we know the dancer from the dance?

W. B. Yeats, "Among School Children"

Introduction:
Moving Imagination to the Center

> Emily is sitting alone at a table with one of her ants in her hand. She is talking to the ant, asking it questions.
>
> Emily: Do you have anything else to say?
>
> She puts her head close to the ant and listens. Later she explains that the ant has been telling her that she's 10 years old, her birthday is August 2, and it's "a her." She shows me how she wrote that information on a piece of paper. (Fieldnotes, September 22)

When I met Emily, she was the first child I had taught who, at 6, had quite plainly begun her life work. Emily is a scientist. It is possible she was born that way, because she is the only 6-year-old I've encountered whose life revolved around a desire to immerse herself exclusively in a study of the natural world. In Emily's case, her chief fascination was with insects, most especially ants. During the year I taught her, she spent all of her outdoor time in fine weather pursuing insects, capturing them, and making containers to keep them in so that she could take them home with her for further observation. As a collector, she was never without plastic baggies. Any crawling thing was scooped up and put in her cubby for later study. She drew the insects and bugs she collected, wrote about them avidly, and offered a wealth of information about most of them to anyone who was interested. She was not, however, a child who ever chose to read a fiction book or listen to a fiction story. She did not involve herself in dramatic play unless I asked her to do so. At home, she insisted on being read only nonfiction, although her parents made valiant attempts to read fiction with her. When left to herself, her interests in life were exclusively in natural science or things that were "real." I was surprised, therefore, to find out early in the schoolyear that Emily believed she could talk to insects (and who am I to say she can't?). Often at recess and sometimes in the classroom she could be seen walking around engaged in serious conversation with whatever poor creature she had happened upon.

PURPOSE OF THE BOOK

We cannot break out into the world of events from within the theoretical world. One must start with the act itself ... not with its theoretical transcription. (Bakhtin, 1993, p. 91)

At the time I taught Emily, I was beginning my third year of inquiry into the subject of imagination and the role it plays in early literacy, and she provided a unique example of the workings of imagination as it interfaced with a specific discipline. Yet Emily was just one child among many who were playing out their imaginative lives in plain view of anyone who cared to watch. This book places the imaginative work of Emily and many other children into a framework that attempts to focus attention on the role of imagination in literacy learning. It will begin with a description of how my questions about imagination emerged, although it will not claim to have answered those questions. I will propose three ways in which I believe imagination is linked to discourse acquisition and forms a cornerstone of the literacy process for students of all ages, presenting data that focus on the issues of identity, discourse appropriation, and what I am calling "authoring." In each of these areas my theoretical structure will be grounded in the "acts" of children, so that the reader can see the recursive way in which my process as a teacher-researcher changed my practice, which in turn changed my theoretical framework, which again changed my process as a teacher-researcher, and so on.

Thus, my descriptions will focus on "the prosaics" (Morson & Emerson, 1990) of imagination. In other words, I will not describe well-planned, teacher-orchestrated artistic events whose goal was to elicit specific imaginative responses to my instruction. Rather, the data will present everyday incidents of imagination I observed and participated in: acts that were part of my own life and the life of the classroom. My purpose in this book, then, is to make tangible the role of imagination as I have seen it working in my classrooms; to open up for discussion the necessity—in fact what I believe to be the imperative—of studying the imaginative work of literacy learners more closely.

It would, however, be the height of hubris for me to claim that by the end of this book the reader will have a definitive description of imagination. Rather, it is quite likely that for some of my readers I may only provoke the sort of disorientation and sense of intangibility that this research has regularly produced in me. To be honest, throughout most of my research process on imagination I could barely make out the image of what I was trying to understand and reach for. There were brief flashes of understanding when I knew for sure that my search was hitting home with children: My data showed me that, the children's achievements showed me that, but then those insights faded into the background. In essence, most of the time my research questions were much too hard. Nonetheless, ever the optimist, I am pushed by my belief in the centrality of imagination to children's work in the world to try to make this elusive process concrete, to point out patterns in what more closely resembles disorder and randomness, and at the same time to propose, as Binet puts it:

> a theory of action, according to which mental life is not at all a rational life, but a chaos of shadow crossed by flashes, something strange and above all discontinuous, which has appeared continuous and rational only because after the event it has been described in a language which brings order and clarity everywhere; but it is a factitious order, a verbal illusion. (Donaldson, 1963, p. 28)

IMAGINATION AND EDUCATION

> In spite of the prevalence of the imagination in life, it is probably true that the discussion of it in that relation is incomparably less frequent and less intelligent than the discussion of it in relation to arts and letters. . . . I suppose that the reason for this is that few people would turn to the imagination knowingly, in life, while few people would turn knowingly to anything else in arts and letters . . . in life the function of imagination is so varied that it is not well defined. (Stevens, 1960, p. 147)

The idea that imagination is a critical part of the educational process is not a new one. At different points in the last century educational theory has embraced the arts, creativity, play, children's questions, and the idea that human intelligence is multidimensional and human expression multimodal (Cadwell, 1997; DeBono, 1969, 1970; Edwards, Gandini, & Forman, 1993; Eisner, 1976; Gardner, 1973, 1980, 1982; Greene, 1995; Heath, 1986; John-Steiner, 1985; Kellogg, 1967; Richardson, 1964). My training as a teacher in the 1970s focused on the methodology being articulated in the British infant schools at that time, in which rich experiences with materials, the importance of play, and the role of the arts in learning were integral. From that base I built a teaching philosophy that placed the arts and creative expression at the center of the curriculum (Gallas, 1994). I have always believed that play is a critical part of learning and wonder is the fuel that feeds our desire to understand the world. These beliefs have shaped my teaching and directed my research.

The use of imagination, therefore, is not new to the field of education or to my practice; yet for educators and researchers it remains, with a few exceptions, a peripheral subject. We know intuitively that imagination is important, but it is difficult to describe how, when, and why it is important. We describe the ways in which teachers can support children's imaginative work and use imagination as a teaching tool, but we do little to describe the workings of the process itself as it relates to our goals. Most often the subject of imagination is approached through discussions of creativity, but imagination remains a mysterious, albeit useful, "dynamic," something that we vaguely know is important to many kinds of creative pursuits. As Brann (1991) points out:

> Even the merely cognitive imagination is . . . a missing mystery in philosophy. This does not mean that the subject is hard to identify in the texts. . . . It is easy to locate the salient and unusually brief passages. . . . It is rather that, when these passages are studied in their contexts, the imagination emerges as an unacknowledged question mark, always the crux yet rarely the theme of inquiry. It is the osmotic membrane between matter and mind, the antechamber between outside and inside, the free zone between the laws of nature and the requirements of reason. It is, in sum, the pivotal power in which are centered those mediating, elevating, transforming functions that are so indispensable to the cognitive process. (p. 32)

Although the subject of imagination has been a peripheral one in the field of education, it has been widely explored by philosophers, artists, theologians, and scientists. Many artists have written explicitly about their imaginative processes (see, e.g., Coleridge, 1907; Grotowski, 1968; Lewis, 1956; Nabokov, 1967; Paz, 1990; Sartre, 1964; Stevens, 1960). Philosophers and theologians have considered the role of imagination in learning and perception, and as a way to situate oneself in the world (see, e.g., Bachelard, 1971; Brann, 1991; Corbin, 1969; de Chardin, 1960; Greene, 1995; Kearney, 1998; Sartre, 1961, 1964; Warnock, 1976). Scientists have spoken or written about the role of imagination in the development of their work (see, e.g., Cobb, 1993; Fox-Keller, 1983; Holton, 1973; Medawar, 1982; Ochs, Jacoby, & Gonzales, 1996; Raymo, 1987; Root-Bernstein, 1989; Salk, 1983; Wolpert & Richards, 1997).

Thus, we have many firsthand accounts of the imaginative process at work in the lives of adults who have achieved fame and success in their respective fields. These accounts are rich with descriptions of the role of imagination. They speak about becoming an expert in a chosen field; about the processes at work in generating important theoretical and experimental breakthroughs; about the connection between the inner world of perception, belief, and identity and the outer world of work and achievement. Rarely, however, are those firsthand insights and theoretical positions taken into account within the field of education, and only recently, in the context of literacy research and teaching, have a few scholars begun to direct their attention to the role of imagination in the process of becoming literate in a discipline (Ballenger, 2003; John-Steiner & Meehan, 1999; Warren, Ballenger, Ogonowski, Rosebery, & Hudicourt-Barnes, 2000).

Of course, the reasons for this omission are obvious. How can one measure and track the imagination? What kinds of verifiable truths might emerge from such an exercise? As Corbin (1969) points out, "The notion that the imagination . . . is an organ of knowledge because it 'creates' being, is not readily compatible with our habits" (p. 180). In the present climate of educational policy, where standardization is the basis upon which curriculum is grounded and test scores provide the measure of a student's success in school, the pursuit of imagination as an educational benchmark seems absurd. I hold the view, however, that the human organism is remarkable precisely because the myriad ways in which it grows and adapts *cannot* finally be quantified. Carini (2001), in her examination of the relation between teaching and learning, writes:

> There is that in learning and thinking, in the teaching-learning relationship, in the process of educating and being educated, which is immeasurable. Immeasurable: not merely not yet measured or simply exceeding our current technological capacity. . . . When the immeasurable isn't recognized or valued, it tends to slip from view. Out of sight, it ceases to claim our minds and attention. We forget how to see it. (pp. 175–176)

RESEARCH DESIGN

Since 1995 I have been attempting to see "the immeasurable" by researching the workings of imagination. Beginning with my own daily experience, then focusing on the children in my primary classrooms, I have used ethnographic methods to collect data on imagination from a variety of perspectives.

(For more on the process of ethnography, see Chapter 8.) My data include my own journal entries, transcripts of audiotapes and interviews with students, artifacts from students' work and play, and fieldnotes from both structured classroom experiences (such as sharing time, science, math, and reading lessons) and more informal expressive times (such as dramatic play, music, art, and block building) when my students chose their own activities. In both formal and informal class time, I acted as a participant-observer, actively taking fieldnotes on an Alpha Smart Pro (a portable word-processing device) and/or audiotaping classroom interactions. During events in which I was directly involved either as a teacher or as a co-actor, my fieldnotes were taken later in the day when I was not teaching, from as little as 30 minutes later to as long as 6 hours. Often, if there were details of physical description or dialogue that I believed were significant and a tape recorder was not on as the event unfolded, I would jot down snatches of conversation on Post-it notes to use as prompts for my later writing. My students knew that I regularly recorded in writing or on tape what they said and did.

Imagination as a Research Tool

While the purpose of my research was to follow the workings of imagination in my classroom, I also found that my exploration of imagination enabled me to use the imaginative process itself as a kind of metacognitive tool. It is no surprise that by closely studying my own imagination I increased my capacity to employ that process as a teacher and a researcher. Thus, I found myself developing a research ethos that incorporated imagination into my stance as a participant-observer and into my point of view as I worked with my data. In later chapters, the reader will see that I made decisions about how to participate in my students' learning from an imaginative standpoint, participating both as a co-learner engaged in a performance and as the teacher engaged in scaffolding young children from one kind of expressive work to another. Further, throughout the process of making sense of what my students were doing, I worked hard to imagine myself into their positions as social actors and students of literacy.

Data Collection in the Classroom

The problem of researching something as intangible as imagination prompted me to begin watching what children were doing in a different way. Instead of identifying a specific question in thinking about literacy, I began simply to look for evidence of imagination wherever and whenever it occurred. One might characterize this as watching for what Dyson (1993) would term the "unofficial" work of children, except that I made new spaces for imagination to emerge in my classroom, thus bringing it into the official realm. I wanted to get a broad picture of imagination. So I changed my practice to accommodate my research question.

Thus, I consciously created a classroom environment where my students had an unusual amount of room to flex their imaginative muscles, as it were, so that I would have opportunities to observe and document their work. There were times when I joined them in their exercises: participating in their dramatic play, painting with them at the easels, joining in their fantasy games, and at all times eavesdropping on their conversations and collecting what they left behind.

The physical design of my classrooms reflected my long-standing belief that elementary classrooms should be richly provisioned and provide many different kinds of spaces for learning and teaching. My classrooms included an extensive library with comfortable pillows and chairs; a writing center supplied with different kinds of papers, labels, envelopes, postcards, greeting cards, pens, and pencils; a math center with manipulatives and games; a science center with plants, animals, rocks, shells, posters, reference books, magnifying glasses, and displays related to our studies; an art and construction center that housed a variety of art materials such as colored pencils and pens, chalk, markers, craypas, paints, clays, brushes, stencils, stamps, papers, glue, paste, felt, pipe cleaners, wire, cardboard, yarn, and materials for collage; a listening center with tapes and books; and a dramatic play area that held costumes, dress-up clothes, house furniture, stuffed animals, and office equipment. There were also active work spaces adjoining one another that encouraged children to eavesdrop and extend their dramatic play and classwork into different areas and media, and quiet work tables where children worked alone or in small groups. The all-purpose materials in the classroom were displayed on open shelves for access; they included resource books, natural materials, and the "tools" of the classroom (rulers, staples, scissors, hole punchers, pencils, and lined and unlined papers).

Although my students did not have assigned desks, they had several cubbies where different kinds of ongoing work were stored. The classrooms also included a large meeting area, usually bordered by a small couch or comfortable chair. In this space whole-class meetings, sharing and group discussions, and small- and large-group instruction took place; group stories and poems were composed; students presented their work; stories were read; and various kinds of manipulative games were played.

The Children

The children whose work will be cited in this book came from two different research settings. Denzel, two of the focal children (Emily and Sophia), and the fourth graders described in Chapter 8 were my students at a large public elementary school in Brookline, Massachusetts, an urban community on the edge of Boston. That school has a culturally, economically, and racially diverse population of more than 550 students. For example, one year we had approximately 32 different languages (and hence nationalities) represented in our K–8 population. (For further description of the school/classes in Brookline, see Gallas, 1994, 1995, 1998.) The remaining children mentioned in this book were students in a small rural school on the central California coast. That school served a relatively homogeneous, middle-class European American population of approximately 150 students in grades K–8.

NOTES ABOUT THE STRUCTURE OF THIS BOOK

This book is not written in a traditional format, either structurally or in terms of its narrative style. Because the book is about imagination, I decided to build a text that reflected the subject I had tackled. As a result, the reader may find the text to be unusual in its presentation, but because I am proposing that imagination can assist us in the process of developing new literacies, I hope the reader will adapt to my design.

The Parts and Frames

This book has four sections, three of which are designated "Parts" and begin with interchapters I am calling "Frames." While writing this book, I realized that there were key texts, or "frames," that helped me decide at different points in my research what, in the face of a lot of confusion and uncertainty, I ought to do or think about next. Thus, the concept of the frame represents a metaphor for me; it is a metacognitive device that propelled this work forward. When I began to think about how this kind of long-term classroom research develops and how to structure my writing for readers, the image that came to me was one of looking through a window frame or camera lens and seeing a landscape I had not seen before. At key points in this research, these frames were texts I "discovered" that gave me the "Aha!" I needed to proceed.

The first frame, which precedes Chapter 2, is from my fieldnotes. Those notes were taken at the end of my year with Denzel, and they pointed me toward studying imagination as a phenomenon. The second frame is a poem I discovered in my fifth year of research that represented for me a complete description of how imagination and literacy are wedded. It helped me in the analysis of my data. The third frame is a journal entry from my travels in Vermont that I had forgotten about and then remembered in the process of considering how imagination is embedded in every glimpse we have of expertise.

The Order of Chapters

The first four chapters in this book were written chronologically. In Chapter 1 we meet Denzel and the problem of story time. This chapter describes the year-long inquiry that led to my study of imagination. In this chapter we also encounter key ideas that I will rely on and refer to in later chapters: multiple literacies, the principle of discourse acquisition, and the distinction between contextualized and decontextualized texts.

Chapter 2 describes how, after my year with Denzel, I began to study imagination systematically in my own life. Using excerpts from my journals, which include data from both personal experience and readings of literary and theoretical works, I started to lay out a framework for understanding imagination and its relation to literacy. In Chapter 3, the study moves back into the classroom, where, 2 years after teaching Denzel, I began to closely observe children's imaginative work

Part II takes what I had learned from my first 3 years of research and breaks the process apart to consider three areas: identity, discourse acquisition, and authoring. Chapter 4 explores how imagination enables a student to achieve a literate identity. Chapter 5 presents a case study of Tommy, a first grader who, like Denzel, had problems becoming engaged with books and stories. It reconsiders the process of discourse acquisition and presents the ways in which I saw it occurring with my students. Chapter 6 introduces the concept of "authoring" by following the work of children in sharing time. It proposes that becoming literate is both a private and a public endeavor.

As I wrote this book, I began to understand more fully the consequences of providing open imaginative spaces for students in the classroom, consequences that move beyond subject-matter competence. Part III explores the possibilities for change and growth that imagination opens up for students and teachers. In Chapter 7, I introduce the idea of sociocultural literacy as an outcome of working with imagination and as a new literacy that healthy classrooms and schools must strive for. Using examples from my first-grade class, I begin to define what the pursuit of sociocultural literacy looks like in one elementary classroom.

Chapter 8 takes a close look at the practical results of reshaping teaching to reflect a commitment to imagination. It considers, first, how the process of classroom ethnography itself relies on imagination to re-envision and improve our teaching. Building on that foundation, I describe a year-long social studies unit to illustrate how curriculum and instruction look in a classroom where imagination is the center. Finally, Chapter 9 explores the paradigm shift that must occur if imagination is placed at the heart of literacy studies.

WHY IMAGINATION?

My desire to understand imagination began with a teaching problem. In 1993 I met Denzel, a second grader. Denzel was a healthy, happy, intelligent child who learned to read in second grade but could not be engaged in listening or responding to literature. I spent one teaching year trying to understand what his lack of engagement meant. At the end of that year, I realized that imagination was a critical part of literacy learning but that I had very little understanding of how it worked.

Denzel helped me see that I wanted to take my students beyond basic skills, to focus less on deciphering codes and more on understanding the deeper contexts within which language is used in every subject. I hope that in the pages to follow the reader will enter the dilemma I encountered with Denzel and see how he offered me an opportunity to examine the ground of my practice; to understand how my ideas about language, teaching, and learning were anchored in an unexamined belief in the importance of imagination as the center of the educational process.

Consider, with me, how failure with a student can be transformed through research into a "Eureka!" moment, how changing what we don't understand into an impossible question can transform our practice. Consider, finally, where imagination fits in our lives: how it affects our learning and development, the learning and development of our students and our own children, the role it plays in the unfolding of our own personal histories. What is imagination? What does it have to do with education? What does it have to do with the outcomes of our students' futures in school and in the world?

CHAPTER 1

Story Time as a Magical Act

When we consult the etymology of the word "read," we find that "read" is lodged in the very guts of the word "ruminate" which means "to think things over." . . . The ruminant's stomach has four compartments, and it is the very last compartment that has gastric glands in its walls for secretion of digestive juices. It is this fourth stomach that is called the read. . . . The anatomy of mystery that lodges explanation in the stomach of the cow suggests that reading was and may still be a ritual of divination, for ritual, in the words of Meyer Fortes, prehends the occult and makes it patent. It seeks what is hidden, internal, unseen in our experience. The reader pores over the text, like the priest reading the entrails, seeking signs of how to live. (Grumet, 1988, p. 133)

As an elementary teacher and the parent of two grown children, I have long accepted the importance of reading storybooks to children from very early childhood on as preparation for the formal reading instruction of the primary classroom. Within my classroom, story time has always been a routine event and a central part of our literacy program. Over the years, though, I had taught many children who had not been read to in their homes. Usually those children struggled with early reading and much of the curriculum in other subjects. Lack of exposure to storybooks loomed large in my mind as a seminal literacy gap. However, until I met 7-year-old Denzel, I had never examined the meaning of storybook reading as a critical literacy event.

THE QUESTION OF STORY TIME

Although normally I have a class of children for 2 years, I taught Denzel for only 1 year. He was 6, going on 7, and was one of the healthiest children I have ever taught. He was not sick, hungry, tired, or hurt. He had no learning disabilities or handicapping conditions. He came to school well dressed, well fed, and well rested, and was much loved by his working-class family. In fact, 10 of his family members lived in his four-bedroom apartment, including his mother and father, brothers, sisters, cousins, and nephews. Denzel knew more about the intricacies of his family tree than I could ever pretend to know about mine.

Denzel was also tremendously serious about school and worked hard to please his teachers. I was surprised, therefore, to realize early in the schoolyear that Denzel and I had a big problem: He couldn't, or wouldn't, listen to stories in our daily read-aloud time. It was a problem that followed us both from September to June of that year. This chapter tells the story of my year-long effort as a teacher to help Denzel understand the purpose of storybook reading, and it also relates my efforts as a teacher-researcher to understand both Denzel's point of view in this process and my own. In this chapter, I take what is a standard feature of early education—that is, story time, or the read-aloud experience—and problematize it, examining what it might tell us about the paths to educational equity, who has access to them, and what our assumptions about the transparency of classroom rituals deny some children.

The events related here, both my interactions with Denzel and my ruminations about how better to serve him, are intended to peel back the layers of this most basic of literacy pursuits. What does it mean to listen to a story being read out loud and look at the pictures in the book? What are the implications for reading and receiving other kinds of texts that are embedded in this activity? What assumptions have we made about the "naturalness" of this activity for children?

> Denzel and I have a problem: He won't listen to story. Won't look at the pictures either. This just makes me crazy. He's a good little kid and I can't for the life of me engage him in story time no matter what book we use or what devices I muster. (Fieldnotes, September 1993)

My inquiry into storybook reading and imagination began with this journal entry early in September 1993 and is culminating, for the time being, in the writing of this book. It is important to point out, though, that my efforts to understand the breakdown between Denzel and myself did not result in a tidy solution for either of us. Denzel never fully participated in story time as a whole-class activity, at least not in a way I could perceive.

I never found a teaching strategy that "fixed" our problem. However, precisely because of that lack of success, I think the story to follow will be instructive. It will magnify the value of teacher research that examines the meanings of habitual practices.

THE SETTING

There were 22 children in Denzel's class, 4 of whom were categorized as non-English speakers. Minority children included East Asians, African Americans, and Latinos. The Asian and European American children were primarily from professional middle- and upper-middle-class families, while the African American and Latino children were from working-class homes. The classroom mix, therefore, offered me quite an unusual population for inquiry about teaching and learning. I had students who had had a solid *mainstream, middle-class preparation for school*: children who had been read two and three books daily since very early childhood, who came in with regular exposure to museums, the arts, and cultural events. With them in the same class were children who spoke little or no English and had just emigrated from foreign countries, some of whom were true immigrants, settling permanently in the United States, and others of whom were here for only a few years while their parents studied in the many institutions of higher education that Boston offered. Rounding out my population were children who were less privileged: children whose families were on public assistance or living in homeless shelters as well as children whose families worked hard but lived on the edge of poverty. Some of these children, though, had also been read to from an early age and had had broad exposure to books and stories; others, like Denzel, had had no book experience and may not have attended kindergarten.

DENZEL AND READING

What, specifically, did Denzel need to learn when we met? From the start, we both agreed that he needed to learn to read. Denzel had not gone to kindergarten, and so his first-grade year had been spent learning prereading skills. Upon entering our school, he began to receive Chapter I reading services as well as individualized instruction in the classroom.

Those interventions continued in second grade during the year I taught him. When Denzel started second grade, he had learned his letters and numbers and some basic phonics skills, and he set out with a vengeance to learn to read. All year, Denzel read and reread the texts we put in front of him, constantly applying newly acquired phonemic and print understandings to the process.

DENZEL AND STORY TIME

Thus, from the day he walked into my classroom, Denzel purposefully learned to read. But in contrast to that seriousness of purpose, at no time was he motivated to *listen* to a story being read to the whole class. If he did not have an adult coaxing him through a story in a one-on-one or small-group situation, carefully laying the context for all the events in the text, Denzel would not attend to the read-aloud experience. Variations in subject matter, narrative style, illustrations, main characters, or any alterations we made in reading strategies and selections of texts—none of these affected his responses. Denzel simply did not seem to be interested in hearing stories read out loud.

For example, in story time when I or another adult would read a book aloud, if the book was not a recently familiar one that he had heard before in a more intimate setting, Denzel would not listen to the story or look at the pictures. He would sit doubled over with his head hidden between his knees, or he would gradually move to the outside of the group and direct his attention to materials on a shelf or the Velcro on his sneakers. Although he was not overtly disrespectful or disruptive, he was clearly impatient with the daily event of storybook reading and often told us so before or after a reading. Further, if we engaged him in conversation about the book in the hope that he'd at least been listening, his remarks indicated that he hadn't heard the story.

By contrast, in sharing time, when members of the class told stories or presented objects to share, Denzel was completely present. He listened carefully, enjoyed the humor and drama of classmates' stories, asked questions, and continued conversations initiated in the sharing-time session throughout the day. Thus, I saw that Denzel could listen, look, and respond to texts presented in a large group, but he seemed to resist the process of responding in similar ways to storybooks. I was quite perplexed. I knew Denzel took reading, books, and his teachers' efforts seriously, but he wasn't able to see the relationship between our whole-class practice of storybook reading and his own goals as a reader.

My earliest reactions to Denzel's behavior ranged from irritation to bewilderment. Because I couldn't characterize his resistance as a challenge to my authority, I examined his ability to listen and attend in other areas. From my own observations, and by all accounts from his other teachers, he was a healthy, eager 7-year-old. I began to question my own reaction to his inattention. Why, I asked myself, was it so important to me that Denzel listen to those stories and look at the pictures? What did I think was happening when children really listened to a story?

My first strategy was to talk to Denzel in an effort to see what he understood about books, asking him whether he was read to at home (he wasn't) and what books were for. Here is one exchange we had. My question was "What are books for?"

> **DENZEL:** *(thinks a long time)* Books make you read more.
> **KAREN:** Books make you read more. But what do you do with them? Why do we even have them?
> **DENZEL:** So you can learn how to read. You look at the books, and so that you know the words. And for little kids to look at the pages.
> **KAREN:** Do grown-ups ever use books? Do you ever see grown-ups using books?
> **DENZEL:** To practice reading. In case they forget some words.

From our conversations I realized that Denzel did not understand the purpose of storybook reading beyond its role in word mastery and thus would not naturally understand the reasons for the read-aloud sessions that occurred each day. Stories—real imaginative fictions that might be worth listening to—were, for Denzel, part of sharing time when he and other children would tell "fake" stories. He was extremely skilled at that activity. Storybooks, however, were not naturally associated with "reading" as he understood it. Reading was where you would "look at the books, and so that you know the words." In the read-aloud situation he could only see the pictures in the book; there was no way he, personally, could follow (and read) the words on the page. Denzel's responses to my questions about books made complete sense within the context of his experience with books, which he saw as utilitarian—a means to an end. How could I transform his understanding of the importance of storybook reading? What did I believe was missing from his interpretation?

STORYBOOK READING AS RITUAL

One day, a few weeks after my conversation with Denzel, I found out from Ann Phillips (a colleague from the Brookline Teacher Research Seminar, who, at my request, had been reading to Denzel once a week) that he thought every book in the classroom was handmade, one by one: hand-copied and hand-bound. As I considered the implications of that misconception, I realized that for children like Denzel, who enter school at age 5 or 6 with no prior exposure to books or intimate reading experiences with family, books, and all events associated with them, must seem mysterious. In fact, the whole event of hearing a story read out loud must seem magical.

Let's just think about it from the point of view of a child who has not been exposed to books before entering school; let's make this taken-for-granted act a little strange. You come to school in kindergarten or first grade, and then this woman you probably haven't known for very long makes everyone sit down on the floor in a group, and she sits up higher, maybe in a tall chair, and everyone else looks up at her and gets quiet. Then she picks up an object, which you know is called a book—but no one has ever told you what a book is or does—and she opens it and holds it up in the air. Words, some of which you've never heard before, begin to come out of her mouth. She points to the pictures and turns the pages, telling a story as she does so. Then she closes the book and puts it back, and the next day at exactly the same time she does the same thing again, but probably with a different book.

If you're an uninitiated participant in this ritualized activity, you're going to think it is quite magical. How does she know the words? Where do the words come from? Where do the pictures come from? In fact, where does the book come from? My questions multiplied, and as they did I realized the deep assumptions I had made about children's understandings of books and the event of story time. I had assumed that all children were like my children, were like me, were like my friends and their children. I had assumed that all children knew that books contained stories and knew how to listen to those stories, that books could be borrowed from libraries or bought in stores.

The Look

> At first glance reading appears to reside within the dominion of the look. Grasped by the look, the words of the text require "image-ination" before they can assume coherence. (Grumet, 1988, p. 129)

At this point, I set about examining what the children in my class who were experienced storybook listeners, the already initiated as it were, did when I or another adult was reading to them. First of all, I noticed that they became very still, their eyes glazed over, their mouths dropped, and they took on what I came to call "The Look." The Look struck me as a slightly zombie-ish state of being mesmerized by the story and the pictures. Pictures were carefully examined. If I moved through the book too fast, there were protests. Often, children requested a second look at a page. As I read, the children did not move for almost the entire story unless there was an exciting or disturbing transition that took place in the plot. At that point I would hear gasps, moans, or squeals. Hands would cover eyes or be clamped over mouths in fear or suspense.

All of these gestures were physical symptoms of being *inside* the story, of using, as Grumet puts it, a process of "image-ination" to bring the story to life. Chapter books without pictures had the same effect. With those, the children looked directly at me as I read even though there were no pictures, and their faces still had The Look. If the books were nonfiction texts, The Look would be slightly different: Brows would be furrowed in concentration, questions would be silently—or sometimes audibly—mouthed, but the bodies would be still, mouths open. So I said to myself, What does The Look mask? What's happening in their heads? And I think I was pretty quick to answer, from my own experience as a reader and listener, that the children were allowing themselves to be transported to another time and place, that they were engaged in an imaginative exercise. In fact, the books *were* magical, producing an altered state of being.

I was getting a better grasp of my motives in wanting Denzel to engage in the receiving of stories. I wanted him to bring the stories to life through his imagination and see the book as having multiple uses in his life. I started to see what wasn't happening for him and tried to talk to him about those things, but by January we hadn't made any significant progress. Finally, in late January, Denzel asked my intern one more time—very pointedly, impatiently, and somewhat desperately as she gathered the class for story time— "Why do I have to listen to story? Couldn't I just read a book by myself?"

She, out of sensible answers (as I was, too, by that time), turned that question back to the children in the class. Here is what they said collectively. This text will offer a further window into what some young children understand about this magical activity. Although Denzel did none of the talking, he was listening.

"Why Do We Listen to Stories?"

MIA: Because, so you can calm down a little after you've been running around, like at recess.

DONNA: It makes, like, your, some of the teachers want your imagination to, like, let go, because sometimes . . .

LATIA: To learn things.

KELLY: To read much better and listen.

NATE: To help you concentrate.

LATIA: If you listen, you'll know how to read the words better because stories have been told to people for centuries and centuries, and the people pass them on, and it calms them down.

CHARLES: It gets them still and interested in what you're reading. Well, I think that, when you listen to a story you can learn new words, and like, you can learn a lot from stories, and people that don't understand things, they can learn words.

MIA: By reading stories you can also tell it to other people, and you can pass it on, and it becomes a big story.

MATT: One story has probably been passed on for centuries and centuries and they change them.

CHARLES: Can you explain that a little more?

MATT: Like, somebody thought of a story, and they passed it on to somebody, and each person changed it a little.

YUAN: I think we read stories because we have to pass things on. Its not like we're immortals or anything, we *have* to pass it on. Just think about how bad the world would be without language, and then just flip it back to stories. 'Cause stories would just die out.

ELI: But you don't *have* to pass them on.

YUAN: But if we forget about stories and how to make them?

ELI: But we could just make new ones.

MATT: But, Eli, if we don't know the old ones, how can we make the new ones?

From this discussion, we can see the nature of the other children's quite sophisticated understanding of story and what its function was in their minds. Stories could transport you; they carried cultural, perhaps even archetypal, knowledge and memory. And they were all intertwined and interrelated.

READING A TEXT

At this point, I began to think again about the word *read,* which we throw around so loosely in this culture. What does it mean to "read" a text? And what, in fact, is a text? For my purposes, I use a definition of *text* that comes from the work of Bakhtin (1986): A text is "any coherent complex of signs ... even the study of art deals with texts" (p. 103). From this vantage point, the words in a children's book are merely one part of the overall text to be read. The pictures are intended to tell more. The children in this class, except for Denzel, habitually scrutinized every picture in the book and had long discussions about the implication of the pictures.

Engaging with Meaning

As I thought more about The Look and talked at length with Denzel about why I wanted him to look at the pictures in the books, I realized that the practice of carefully "reading" pictures is essential for mastery of many subjects at higher levels. For example, when we look at a painting, we are "reading" a text; when studying biology, we "read" the slides under the microscope; we learn to "read" maps, graphs, music, and equations. Each of those readings gives us a different kind of knowledge. There are probably many more examples of texts that could be mentioned, but the point remains that in all of these readings, we must learn to take meaning from a text. Further, in many of these readings we are projecting ourselves into another space, another time, another framework. To read a text with understanding and insight, we must move inside the text, pulling our life along with us and incorporating the text and our lives into a new understanding of the world. Anything less is not a complete and informed reading. Anything less is just peeking, or browsing, or dallying with a text. I realized that I wanted Denzel to get The Look because The Look meant something deeper. It meant that he might use his imagination and the text to move to places he had not been, to read himself into worlds and discourses he would need to master.

My standoff with Denzel over story time played itself out all over the curriculum all through the year. When, for example, we studied Native Americans for several weeks, Denzel never fully embraced and involved himself in the study, remaining cooperative but detached from our work. As with story time, he was physically present and well behaved, but he was unable to take advantage of the many reference books and artifacts we had gathered as resources for his own learning. In math, when presented with manipulative materials such as Cuisinaire rods, whose specific application to mathematics was not obvious, Denzel remained distant and skeptical, voicing his opinion that they were not "real math." At different times in the year, when presented in science with an observation task that focused on an unfamiliar organism or event, Denzel seemed unable even to see in front of him the phenomenon to be observed. This kind of separation occurred in virtually every subject, and we labored together, with inconsistent results, to figure out my intentions as his teacher and the uses that other kinds of "texts" might have for Denzel as a learner.

Reading Versus Storytelling

Evidence from researchers on early literacy has shown that children bring different social and cultural understandings of print to school (Cochran-Smith, 1984; Goelman, Oberg, & Smith, 1984; Heath, 1982, 1983, 1986; Heath & Thomas, 1984; Ninio & Bruner, 1976; Scollon & Scollon, 1981; Smagorinsky, 2001; Taylor, 1983; Teale, 1986; Wolf & Heath, 1992). These studies show that introductions to literature and story are social processes, framed, orchestrated, and scaffolded by the parents and the family in ways that reflect not one pervasive cultural understanding of story but specific cultural orientations that may or may not resonate with that of the school. For students in schools, different literacy events can be characterized as being either familiar, and therefore embedded in the events of everyday life (*contextualized*), or unfamiliar, and therefore disembedded or separate from the events of daily life (*decontextualized*). Signs, shopping lists, notes, letters, and directions are all examples of contextualized print that children see used in their daily lives. For some children like Denzel, however, storybooks are decontextualized because they are not used or even seen in the home.

As we know from Heath's (1983) study of the community of Trackton, stories for the African American children in that community were embedded in the close social networks of family and friendship, while reading was used to further the day-to-day functioning of home, neighborhood, and work. Reading, for the Trackton children, was instrumental and contextualized, and the transition to school presented them with completely different "notions of truth, style, and language appropriate to a 'story'" (p. 294). Denzel's understanding of reading and story time reflects a similar dichotomy: Books were for learning how to read better, but stories were dramatic performances that furthered social interactions among friends. Story time fell into the category of reading and books, while stories themselves were exchanged in sharing time or among friends.

Rosenblatt (1978), in describing how readers approach texts, contrasts "efferent" and "aesthetic" readings, and these categories add further distinctions to the notion of contextualized and decontextualized texts. The efferent reader "concentrates on what the symbols designate, what they may be contributing to the end result that he seeks," while the aesthetic reader's "primary purpose is fulfilled during the reading event, as he fixes his attention on the actual experience he is living through" (p. 27). Her contrasts call up for me the contrasting images of Denzel and the other children in my class. Denzel is disengaged, looking only to master the mechanics of reading ("what the symbols designate") and listening only to learn practical information about how to read, if there is any.

The other children in my class, however, caught within the grasp of The Look, are, indeed, "living through" the events of the text. Their engagement is evocative of Coleridge's "willing suspension of disbelief" (Coleridge, 1907, p. 6), a position that places trust in the ability of texts to expand our experience of the world from the utilitarian to the transcendent. It is an act of imagination, synthesizing memory, psyche, emotion, and logic into a new vision of the world. That position was not one that Denzel could take.

WHAT IS LITERACY?

The art of listening to stories is basic training for the imagination (Frye, 1964, p. 116).

As a teacher, I cling firmly to the belief that every student who walks into my classroom should be offered the opportunity to engage deeply in the content and process of every discipline. To put it another way, I want each student I teach to begin acquiring the many different discourses that will make him or her successful in school and in life. *This is a multiple literacy, or multiliteracies, approach to schooling that proposes that there are many reading, writing, and speaking systems, each of which requires different kinds of expressive and receptive language learning* (Gee, 1996; Hull & Schultz, 2001; Moll, 1992; New London Group, 1996; Scribner & Cole, 1981; Street, 1993, 1995). Some of those systems are learned in school. Others are learned at home or through the many communication systems now available, such as the Internet. Within this framework, I believe that the process of education in schools, from kindergarten through graduate school, is one of working to master, or acquire, different discourses at increasing levels of complexity.

Discourse Acquisition

For me, then, discourse acquisition is the linchpin of schooling; it is the point at which real educational equity occurs. It is more than, for example, learning the names and dates of events in history or regurgitating the main themes in a short story. It is more than sitting through a 50-minute class three times a week and taking notes. It is a way of being in the world: learning to walk, talk, write, think, and perhaps even dream like a historian, a writer, a mathematician, an artist, or a scientist. The more ways of being we acquire, the more discourses we master, the more easily we move through different strata of society and the world.

Within this framework, I see myself as the initiator of the discourse acquisition process for my students. But, to be realistic, the process of discourse acquisition that I have just described is a complex and intricately constructed corpus. My questions and reflections about the purposes of storybook reading during my year with Denzel led me to believe that the process of remaining open and curious about the meaning of a text is a critical factor in the process of discourse acquisition and the achievement of full literacy across a wide variety of subjects. Full literacy to me implies an ability to work with all kinds of texts, especially those that seem odd or unfamiliar. To be open to what a text offers depends on the action of the imagination.

Bridging Skills and Understanding

With consistent drill and practice, Denzel mastered the basic skills of reading and writing, but I knew that this was an intelligent, serious student for whom I was not building the bridge between skill and depth of understanding; I was not moving him from dabbling in a discourse to full engagement with it. As Edwards and Mercer (1987) point out, "learning failures ... are failures of context" (p. 167). My failure in Denzel's case was a failure of purpose. In other words, in our time together Denzel never understood the purpose of storybook reading in the larger picture of his possible life history: I was not able to lay a powerful enough context to persuade him to enter the worlds that good literature might open up for him and, by implication, to help him engage in other kinds of texts that would open other worlds of experience and understanding.

As the year ended, I did understand more about why that didn't happen between us. At the core of our failure was my inability to comprehend the nature of Denzel's imaginal world, to see what he was bringing to our collaboration and, in doing so, to find ways to bring him into the world of the storybook and the different discourse it represented. But although that realization came too late for Denzel and me, it forced me to reconfigure my classroom approach to storybook reading, and it also set me on another path of investigation. I began to consider how to gain access to children's imaginal worlds, how to help bridge the gap between their "now" and the new worlds of the texts I wanted them to enter. In essence, as a teacher-researcher, although I initially focused on a specific problem because of my inability to reach and understand one child, that focus changed the way I teach all children. The stories of those children and what they also taught me about imagination and literacy are told in the chapters that follow.

PART I

The Question

FRAME

"Look, Karen, I'm Running Like Jell-O!"

My fieldnotes from the final days of school revealed how, after 9 months of inquiry into storybook reading that seemed to reach a dead end, I was able to see something I had not seen before, something that helped me focus in on imagination as the phenomenon I needed to study. These fieldnotes were written consecutively through the week.

Monday, June 16:
I've been very distracted by Denzel and what I perceive to be some kind of failure on our part (his and mine) to crack this thing called school. I want to feel like he has entered the metadiscourse on thinking and learning that the other children move so freely through—the one that combines intellect and creativity, that uses imagination to enter new subjects, or books, or poems—I don't feel that I've gotten him to that point where my knowledge of higher-order thinking, and how one accesses that, is available to him. What is it that I want from him? It seems to be a particular kind of mindfulness. How to define it?

Tuesday:
We have our "summer-baby-birthday-party." Parents bring in great food: sushi, cake and strawberries, cookies, cupcakes, juice, and Jell-O.

Ayako's mom made a raspberry Jell-O that was just beautiful: layers of white and red gelatin. Denzel had four servings. We went outside to play, and half the class started to make up a line game that sort of resembled Red Rover but was a line that, like an ocean wave, chased and then enclosed whomever it caught. They were chanting nonsense rhymes, laughing and falling. Denzel and Alex came out a little late, and they watched them for a few seconds; then Denzel came over and asked me if he could go and play catch with his cousin, who was also out on the playground with his class. I said "no," that I wanted him to play with our class. He shrugged, pulled his hood up over his head, and walked reluctantly over to the galloping line. When he got there, the line began to break into fours and threes. He stood silently, not joining any group. I called out to Mark, "Look, Mark, there's some children who have just come out! Can you tell them what you're doing?" Mark called back, "Sure!" as he galloped past, and I urged Denzel and Alex to follow him. They did so slowly, obviously not feeling invited but trying to please me.

The children went under a big pine tree that was shady and con-ferred. Denzel stood on the edge of the group. Then the group broke apart, running in goofy ways, making nonsense sounds. Denzel watched them for a minute, then followed, running in a jerky, wobbling manner past me, and he had a big smile on his face and called out, "Look, Karen, I'm running like Jell-O!" He continued running after the group, then reached them and ran on. I stood still, trying to grasp the words, shocked at the metaphor that had just come out of his mouth. Had I ever heard him use a metaphor before? I don't think so.

Wednesday:
I watched Denzel playing soccer with a group of boys using the entire playing field, which is huge, for their game. At one point Denzel was skipping backwards, anticipating the arrival of the ball . . . as fast as he could with no one in sight. Then he tripped, fell, rolled over once backwards, jumped up with a huge smile on his face, and continued skipping backwards.

What's happening in your head?, I thought. What do you think about when you are in the middle of a pure movement sequence? Is it like the middle of drawing a picture, or doing a dance, or writing a poem, or singing a song? Is it like being in the middle of a story? What is happening in your head? Are you imagining or reimagining yourself in another place and time and piece of your life?

Thursday:
The last day of school. We usually have a private class recital. That
means that anyone who wants to perform, can. Children dance, sing,
play instruments, do impersonations. There are many surprises. When
I asked in the morning who wanted to perform, about half the class
responded, including Denzel. My intern, Cindy, and I surveyed what
the children would be doing. Denzel said he would be doing a dance.
That afternoon we gathered in the auditorium, sitting in two levels of
chairs around the piano. As always, different children surprised and
delighted us. When Denzel's turn came, he got up, went to the center
of the empty space, and announced, "I will do a dance from karate.
And it's called 'The Lion.' But I won't do the song."

He then performed a beautiful series of movements beginning
with a crouch, transitioning to back rolls and somersaults that propelled him around the edges of the audience in an arc. Then he
sprang up onto all fours and crawled slowly across the center of the
space growling in a low, even . . . Was it a purr? A lion's purr? Our
mouths dropped at this, and the children, who had been absolutely
silent and still, bent forward imperceptibly to see him, wondering,
as I was, I think, whether they were hearing things! Finally Denzel
stopped, dropped lower to the floor, and then raised himself up on
his knees with his hands resting on his lap. "Done," he said. We
applauded, still somewhere between wonder and bewilderment.
Then Denzel announced, "The Snake." He began again, a less choreo-
graphed version of the movement of the snake, including more rolls,
half-somersaults, a dance clearly emerging from the martial arts. But
this one seemed different from the first. I could have sworn he was
improvising.

From these notes taken in my last week of school with Denzel, I saw what
should have been obvious to me throughout the year: Imagination was
there working for Denzel on a sophisticated, aesthetic, and intellectual level.
To Denzel, movement was a way to imaginatively understand his world, one
I had missed in spite of careful watching and talking for 9 months. It
occurred to me that our inability to solve the problem of story time was
grounded in my lack of knowledge about how imagination worked.
Although I professed to be a teacher who enabled children to use their
imaginations to further their learning, I had only a superficial understanding of imagination, one I had never examined. From these notes, I
immediately saw what I needed to do next.

CHAPTER 2

Imagination as a Question, a Topic, a Tool

Everything man does that's worth doing is some kind of construction, and the imagination is the constructive power of the mind set free to work on pure construction for its own sake. The units don't have to be words; they can be numbers or tones or colors or bricks or pieces of marble. It is hardly possible to understand what the imagination is doing with words without seeing how it operates with some of these other units. (Frye, 1964, p. 119)

After that last week of school, my questions emerged more clearly. What does imagination look like in its different forms? Where does it fit in the process of literacy learning and teaching? How does one pursue a study of something as permeable as imagination? As Frye points out, in order to begin to "understand what imagination was doing with words," I needed to broaden my notion of the forms it took in everyday life. Since those last days of June 1994, I have been trying to develop an understanding of imagination that focuses on those questions. In 1994–1995, when I was not teaching, I began to consider imagination as a topic to be investigated, and I realized that I had to begin with my own life. This chapter lays out the development of my first efforts to learn more about imagination in the year following my work with Denzel. It includes a description of the research process that emerged for me: a process of reading, writing, and self-conscious reflection.

BEGINNING WITH MYSELF

In July of 1994, I started a year-long journal about my own experiences of imagination, using the journal as a tool to focus in on the problem of expanding how I viewed imagination. I contemplated, for example, the problem of understanding pure movement as an imaginative form, recording what passed through my mind when I took my daily 2-hour walk, when I danced, when I swam; I recorded my thinking about reading literature and listening to music, about reading and writing poetry. Slowly, I became more aware of the silent, almost autonomic thinking that accompanies the actions I engaged in in my daily life. During this process I forced myself to consciously record what I was thinking when it finally made itself known to me. For example, in early December, as I walked along a desolate stretch of coast, the following words popped into my head, and after they ran on for a while I noticed them, stopped walking, and wrote them down as fast as I could in the little pocket journal I had taken to carrying:

> Once this coast was common land, covered only by spanses of wooly briars, old man's beard, bursting clouds of filament, wily oaks, and crackling bittersweet. They ran from the edge of the beaches, just behind the tufts of sea grass, straight across hills of granite and pine— forever. The only way in was from the rocky coast, and it offered no knowledge of how to pass through. There were no paths, only deer run and the low, damp tunnels of ancient box turtles. In this land, I live, with little memory or imagination. My sight of that time is limited to night frights and small moments of delight in the objects cast off by the ocean.
>
> That is only partly true. There is a quality of imagination that admits me to other worlds, that begins stories about things or people I see, and lets me begin to build their story around some random (or purposeful?) act, one I only happen upon. But those stories are only beginnings. . . . And besides they only unfold in my head. The texts are never more than vines of story, starting and stopping, then unwinding in quieter hours.

I soon found that this practice of recording made what had formerly been an unconscious process more available to me. What I began to see were the different ways in which imagination permeated my inner life.

Reading

> "There'll be apples on those trees in a few weeks," remarked the minstrel, looking up at the branches overhead, where the first buds were fattening toward their sweet annual explosion into white. (Babbit, 1969, p. 61)

One day in November, reading this passage from *The Search for Delicious* (Babbit, 1969), I realized I was caught in the book: I felt the spring, the warming earth and air. I saw the bursting blossoms, knew the scent of nectar and pollen. I held the perception of both bud and blossom in my mind as a complete whole. I was struck by how that happened for me as a reader. Could it have happened, I wondered, if I had never been in an apple orchard in spring? Would Denzel have experienced that passage in the same way?

When I used my imagination as a reader, I suspected that I needed to have had that sensory experience of place and blossoming fruit trees to imagine and comprehend the feeling Babbit's text was evoking and that that flash of understanding, memory, and aesthetic response occurred in the moment I was reading the text. I found myself living inside the text, unconsciously cross-referencing it with my life experience. I did not constantly stop in the course of reading to find a context from which to relate to the text, although I knew my reading was often interrupted as I allowed myself to savor the imagery and sensations a particular passage had evoked.

Writing

Similarly, one day in late October I spotted a dead seal on the beach, and, over the course of the next few days, I observed it carefully. About a week later, I wrote a poem describing my observations, part of which follows:

Seal at Brace's Cove

When she washed up we had a short conversation
a word or two expressing my regrets.
She was no longer inside that body, I knew that
could tell it by her empty eyes and tongueless jaws.
But her swimming form was there
the delicacy of her still poised flippers
the roll of her belly as she took the swell.
Next day the tide pulled her back
I looked for her and knew she was floating in the cove.
The wind came up two days or more
then the ocean gave her up again.
She waited for me patiently, resting on the upmost rocks.

> We talk everyday and sometimes we sing together
> and sometimes I sing alone and wonder
> what kind of joy is this for conversation with carrion?
> But beneath the flies and hidden creatures searching her body
> there is the beauty of a life
> of floating and diving and surrendering to currents
> of seal pups and more.

When I saw the seal on the beach, I was fascinated by it and examined it—not to know how it looked, because I did know that, but to piece together what had happened to it, where it had come from, how it had died, how long it had been dead. I found myself creating a scenario based on what I could observe and what I could imagine. As the poem conveys, I was surprised at how my visits to the seal took on the flavor of a "conversation with carrion."

I have never been a seal, but I've seen them in the ocean and in captivity. I know their habits, how they look and sound, what they eat. As a child and adolescent, I spent a great deal of time swimming in the open ocean far from shore and body-surfing in the waves off the coasts of California and Hawaii. Could I have written that poem if I'd never seen a seal before or had not experienced the ocean and the tides as a swimmer? Could I have placed the seal there and imagined its death? Again, the question of real-life experience inserted itself into my efforts to understand how my imagination worked.

Reaching for the Infinite

Paired with that question was a growing sense that my imaginative responses to real-life experiences had another dimension. By mid-December, I had identified a dilemma in my research that I couldn't avoid, one that naturally forced itself upon me as I kept track of imagination.

> I have the sense that I want to explore the divine. Even when I contemplate nature, dead seals, a sunset, it is from a point of wonder and awe—a desire to experience, reexperience, and track the presence of divinity around me. . . . I think I am in search of a way to understand how some experiences in the world lead to glimpses of joy, ecstasy,

the divine. But the way into that understanding is a seeming black hole that yields no light: I arrive at the moment breathless and without gravity, like the untethered astronaut in the film *2001,* floating off into a dark, lifeless void. Is this where the search for the divine begins? (Journal entry, December 19)

In January, as I continued to search for theoretical work on imagination, I encountered *The Divine Milieu,* by Teilhard de Chardin (1960). In that work, de Chardin explores how investigations into science and the origins of matter evoke a sense of wonder and mystery as we contemplate the evolutionary process and the complexity of the natural world:

> Where are the roots of our being? In the first place, they plunge back and down into the unfathomable past. How great is the mystery of the first cells which were one day animated by the breath of our souls! How impossible to decipher the synthesis of successive influences in which we are for ever incorporated! In each one of us, through matter, the whole history of the world in part reflected. (p. 27)

De Chardin's reflections on the sense of mystery and wonder evoked when one closely examines the natural world mirrored my growing awareness of the ways in which, for me, an examination of even the smallest phenomenon in nature often resulted in astonishment and awe.

I recalled how this kind of wonder was something I sought to convey to the children I taught through science, not from a conscious desire to make them more spiritual beings, because that conflicted mightily with the parameters of what teachers in public schools are charged to do, but rather because wonder and awe are such a natural offshoot of open inquiry into the sciences. And, as de Chardin points out, wonder and awe emanate from our realization that we are incapable of understanding the immense complexity that surrounds us:

> Our mind is perplexed when we try to plumb the depths of the world beneath us. But it reels still more when we try to number the favorable chances which must conjoin at every moment if the least of living things is to survive and succeed. (p. 49)

Thus, the study of science presents a contradiction: We strive to expand our understanding of the world at the same time that we see, and celebrate, the limitations of our understanding.

Next, I encountered the work of Ralph Waldo Emerson (1849/1983), writing at an earlier time in history about his perception of the natural world:

> The method of nature: who could ever analyze it? That rushing stream will not stop to be observed. We can never surprise nature in a corner; never find the end of a thread; never tell where to set the first stone. The bird hastens to lay her first egg; the egg hastens to be a bird. The wholeness we admire in the order of the world, is the result of infinite distribution. Its smoothness is the smoothness of the pitch of the cataract. Its permanence is a perpetual inchoation. Every natural fact is an emanation, and that from which it emanates is an emanation also, and from every emanation is a new emanation. (p. 118)

I recalled, as I read this passage, how I had observed in the work of young children the same awareness of the circularity in creation. As a first grader, one of my former students had written in her science journal, "How everything is made. It is very hard. It was very hard to make something because it would have to take a 1000. Like a watermelon. Something made that and something before made that, and on and on forever." (See Figure 2.1.) Her accompanying drawing, as a rendering of what she was trying to express, offers a further look at her thinking and her sense that she was pondering a difficult abstraction. We see that she draws lines to imagine the development through time of living things, not a linear progression, but a moving one. As another drawing, "How the World Became" (Figure 2.2), signals, many of the young children I have taught have wondered about, but could not have understood or articulated as Emerson and de Chardin did, the complexity and variability that characterizes the natural world. Their simple expressions, however, reflect an imaginative projection of wonder and questioning about what they were perceiving in their environment.

All of these thinkers, children and adults alike, had a common starting point. Each began with an openness to a moment in time; each perceived and wondered at the immensity of creation. Emerson (1849/1983) writes:

> Crossing a bare common, in snow puddles, at twilight under a clouded sky, without having in my thoughts any occurrence of good fortune, I have enjoyed a perfect exhilaration. I am glad to the brink of fear. . . . Standing on the bare ground, my head bathed by the blithe air and uplifted into infinite space,—all mean egotism vanishes. I become a transparent eyeball; I am nothing; I see all. (p. 10)

HAO AVR e IS
MAD A IS VAR e HIRD
At WIS VAR e HIRD
To MK SIM HeN B KIS
At WD HAS TAKA
LOD O

FIGURE 2.1. "How everything is made"

I saw that all of these responses to experience began with a childlike openness to the world. Cobb (1993) proposes that such moments in childhood
are grounded in the sense of wonder—what she calls "the ecology of imagination." They are marked in the individual's memory at the time as being
significant and full of deeper meaning.

I believe that this openness, this imaginative surrender to a particular
moment of experience, is a prerequisite for deep engagement with the arts

and the sciences: Imagination feeds our ability to ask the big questions, to think large and deep, "to be glad to the brink of fear" (Emerson, 1849/1983, p. 10). But imagining such infinity, such endless variation, is potentially frightening, uncertain, precarious. We, children and adults alike, can lose our anchors in the world when faced with the enormity of the mystery. It is much easier to avoid the power of that kind of engagement, to avoid the questions it evokes and the uncertainty it requires.

IMAGINATION AS A TOOL

This kind of reading and reflection represents a part of what I was trying to do during that year. By studying my own experience of imagination and beginning to read the works of others who had inquired into the subject, I felt I could start to pull the phenomenon apart and develop new categories within it. In fact, over the year I did identify a number of different ways in which my imagination was functioning in my inner life, recording examples over time of fantasies, delusions, wonder and questioning, play, dreams, song lines, movement patterns, fears, visualizations, projections, and more. I also discovered the ways in which those functions had positive or negative effects on my daily life and on my own learning. The following excerpt from my journal illustrates a case in which my imagination interfered with

FIGURE 2.2. "How the world became"

my learning. In this case I was having my first class using scuba-diving equipment in water.

> Although I had wanted to learn for a long time, every now and then a bit of panic would seize me as the thought of not being completely in atmosphere (that is, breathing air naturally) passed through my mind. What I was aware of was the lack of control in the endeavor. In other words, if everything went well this new pastime was a snap; but if something went wrong. . . . Well, my imagination ran amok with the possibilities . . . overrunning logic; the whole thing had hints of mortality about it. I was fine until I went down (below the surface), breathing as I'd been taught, but the quality of the breaths was alarming. There wasn't enough air, just as I'd imagined. I became claustrophobic and signaled that I had to surface.

By the end of that year, there were few aspects of my daily life I could name that were not influenced by imagination. For example, at their most basic levels, the functions of the autonomic nervous system—breathing, swallowing, digestion, the beating of our hearts, the blinking of our eyes— are not governed by the work of the imagination. However, on further consideration it becomes clear that these functions, if acted on by the conscious or subconscious mind, can be altered by the action of imagination. Hence the emergence of different body–mind practices, such as yoga, meditation, and biofeedback, and the existence of such psychosocial disorders as anorexia nervosa and post-traumatic stress disorder. Essentially, even the simple act of walking down a street requires a form of imaginative projection to bring itself to completion: We must first develop a goal that is to be achieved in the future (taking a walk), plan the route of the walk, predict the weather conditions and dress accordingly, anticipate the hazards on the street, and, finally, remember to take along the key to the house so that on our return we are not locked out. None of these functions—planning, predicting, anticipating, applying, and remembering—can occur effectively without the work of the imagination.

IMAGINATION AS A TOPIC

For the purposes of thinking about Denzel and my original questions, though, I continued to explore how imagination was conceptualized on a theoretical level in different disciplines, reading firsthand accounts of imaginative work by artists and scientists as well as theoretical works on imagination in the fields of literature, psychology, and philosophy. I found the works of Warnock (1976), Sartre (1961), and Cobb (1993) to be especially helpful as I reconsidered the relationship of imagination to learning. Sartre (1961), for example, describes the way in which "imaginative knowledge" interacts with the world:

> Imagination is not an empirical and superadded power of consciousness, it is the whole of consciousness as it realizes its freedom; every concrete and real situation of consciousness in the world is big with imagination. (p. 270)

Within this definition, Sartre proposed that to comprehend events in the world—whether reading a novel, viewing a painting, or participating in a mundane daily event—there must be a movement back and forth between the real and the imaginary. Thus, the mind apprehends the present by association with the past. However, Sartre's conceptualization of imagination underscored the tension that existed for me in attempting to define and study imagination. In his framework, imagination represents both freedom from reality and dependence on reality for its meaning. Artworks, novels, poems, performances become "analogues" that convey meaning using reference points that are from lived experience but are not real themselves (p. 277).

Thus, to imagine something one must know it in some way in the world; to comprehend events in the world, one must use imagination as a reference point. We move back and forth between consciousness and the "hidden surpassing towards the imaginary" (Sartre, 1961, p. 273). Images take us to new levels of understanding, but our apprehension of them is constituted by real experience:

> It is the image which is the intuitive "filling in" of the meaning. If I think "sparrow," for instance, I may at first have only a word and an empty meaning in my mind. If the image appears, a new synthesis is formed and the empty meaning becomes a consciousness full of *sparrow.* (Sartre, 1961, p. 83; emphasis in original)

Warnock (1976) speaks to another aspect of imagination, that of interpretation and its relationship to perception. She emphasizes the importance of imagination to the process of finding meaning in unfamiliar symbolic objects:

> We use imagination in our ordinary perception of the world. This percep-
> tion cannot be separated from interpretation. Interpretation can be common
> to everyone, and in this sense ordinary, or it can be inventive, personal, and
> revolutionary. So imagination is necessary to enable us to recognize things
> in the world as familiar, to take for granted features of the world which we
> need to take for granted and rely on if we are to go about our ordinary busi-
> ness; but it is also necessary if we are to see the world as significant of some-
> thing unfamiliar, if we are ever to treat the objects of perception as symbol-
> izing or suggesting things other than themselves. (p. 10)

Thus, imagination is both mundane and transcendent. It reflects our experiences back to us in recognizable forms and images that do not surprise
or alarm us, but it also creates unique representations of that same experience whose form and image suggest that our experience has dimensions
beyond those we have perceived.

Cobb (1993) uses a framework of human ecology to describe the development of imagination. She views imagination as a "bioaesthetic striving"
in which "the child must transcend nature psychologically and semantically
before he can know the nature he perceives in cultural (ie, human) terms"
(p. 18). Cobb's extensive review of the role of imagination in the development of artists and scientists offered me a rich context from which to consider how close contact with the natural world sustains the sense of wonder throughout the life cycle.

BACK TO DENZEL

What, if anything, does this work tell me about Denzel? I recall sitting with
him one afternoon in front of a tank full of newts and pond plants. That
day I had asked all the children in the class to do an observation drawing
and written entry in their science journals. Some children were observing
caterpillars, some the cockatiels, some the fish in the tank, some the bunny.
Denzel had chosen to observe the newts, but, looking into the tank, he was
unable to see them or describe what they were doing, even after I tracked
their movement on the glass of the tank with my finger. (They were swimming, sitting on top of each other, floating at the surface—all common newt
behavior.) So observation, the process of gathering data, was a blocked point,
a rupture, maybe because he didn't understand the purpose of "looking."
(For more development of this idea of rupture in the teaching and learning

process, see Chapter 8.) And there I am, back to my dilemma of a year earlier: the storybook, the text, the picture, the question of imagination and how to read ourselves into the word and the world (Freire & Macedo, 1987).

At the end of that year, my reading and my documentation of my imaginative process had broadened my ability to look back at Denzel, to better understand the points at which he had and had not made contact with storybooks and other kinds of classroom texts, and to clarify my observations about my own imagination. In fact, in looking back over my notes on Denzel's work, I realized that during our year together I had overlooked two pieces of data about his imaginative world. One aspect that I discovered in my fieldnotes began to occur around November of my year with him in the area of Science Talks (Gallas, 1995). After a few months of experience with Science Talks, Denzel began to ask amazing questions about the world: "Why is grass green? How is glass made? How do babies grow inside the mother?" Before my study of imagination, I had always seen these questions as representing a distinct process that was essential to the study of science, that of wonder. But until I began to think deeply about imagination, I did not define *wonder* as one kind of imaginative process among many.

Now I see that wonder is a subcategory of imagination that Denzel regularly worked with in school, both in his sharing-time stories and in our talking about science. While he could not work with "texts" as resources that would enable him to be engaged with science study in a visual and physical way, he could engage in scientific discourse in the hypothetical mode, just as he could engage with story as an imaginative proposition through storytelling.

I also revisited the one stunning occasion in the 9 months I taught Denzel when he did let go of the real and entered the imaginative plot of a storybook. When that event occurred, I considered it an isolated anomaly because it did not recur on other occasions. One day, early in June, I read *Heckedy Peg,* by Audrey and Don Wood (1987). *Heckedy Peg* presents an archetypal situation found in many fairy tales: A poor mother leaves her seven children alone in the house while she makes her weekly visit to the market, instructing them as she leaves to be good children, not to let strangers in the house, and not to play with fire. Of course the children break her rules and are persuaded by Heckedy Peg, a witch, to let her in the house and light her pipe. In return, she changes the children into food and takes them home for her supper.

When the good mother returns home to find her children gone, she is led to the witch's hut by a blackbird who has observed the seduction and kidnapping. The mother—loving, courageous, and intelligent—rescues her children and chases the witch away. There is no mention of punishment or lessons learned, but the lesson was palpable on my second graders' faces as they listened and in their comments as they discussed the book. For the first and only time that year, Denzel spent the entire reading on his knees, eyes wide, mouth open, and The Look of imaginative transcendence on his face! As the story ended, he was excited and astonished at the children's disobedience, and he was also proud that, as he said, "Mothers could be that brave. My mother is!" It was as if a tiny window had opened for him, showing what literature might offer, a window that could open because of Denzel's close relationship with his own mother. Denzel's entry into that story unleashed his own stories about his mother and her steadfastness; it also allowed him to see his mother in the context of another time and place. But this was one lone occasion in a year of readings.

I realize now that my sense of failure with Denzel was, in part, due to my inability to see the steps he was making. I was expecting the form and content of his imaginative work to mimic or mirror mine. In fact, it was because we were so different that I perceived our interactions as being without real gains. I couldn't then, and still can't, picture how he reimagined and thus reconceptualized the experiences he was having in class, but clearly, from my data, I can see that he was involved in that process.

What I did gain from my year of study and inquiry, though, was a sense of the vast sweep of imagination in my life, and I knew I had never looked at children's uses of imagination with a real consciousness of its breadth of influence over daily life and learning. The next step, therefore, was to observe imagination in the classroom. The following chapter describes what I saw when I began that process.

CHAPTER 3

Observing Imagination

The blocks fall and the girls laugh and scream, "Wrecked neighbor-hood! Wrecked neighborhood! Wrecked neighborhood!" It sounds just like the boys in the blocks. Peter and Tommy, who are building with Cuisinaire rods, look over and laugh approvingly. Chinua and Nat are at the clay table, building towers. They are conversing about the tow-ers, "Empire engineer number nine, lift it!" Sonny, Donaldo, and Brian pick up the chant in the art area, where they are painting, swooping paint across the paper as they do. Betty and Emily are at a round table making a list for me of things they think I need in the drama center. Betty says, "What's the sound at the end of *pants?*" The entire class is involved in building, making, pretending. No exceptions. (Fieldnotes, September 28)

In September I returned to teaching, delighted to find that my first-grade students were some of the most creative children I had ever taught. (Or one might propose that my new focus on imagination as a teacher-researcher affected both my perception of the characteristics of my students and their behavior. Suffice it to say that I perceived at the time that these children were marvelously imaginative.) Following on my work from the previous year, my desire to broadly observe imagination in my classroom, and my real-ization through Denzel that I needed to expand the opportunities for my students to work with retellings of stories, I allotted much more time in the afternoons for the children to work with the visual arts and music, to explore creative dramatics in the block corner and the drama center (which included props, puppets, and various materials for costumes), and to pur-sue their own projects.

I had found in the past that some children would naturally confine themselves to choosing one medium exclusively. Thus, I also made sure that the children sampled all of the expressive opportunities in the classroom, over the course of a week, rather than allowing them a free choice every day. At the same time, I began a year-long project of asking the children to dramatize the stories we read during story time. This part of the chapter will describe what I saw and heard, looking at the children's work in the more open-ended afternoons as well as within different subjects.

FROM PLAYING TO DRAWING TO WRITING

> Today at recess as we were lining up to go in the classroom, my pen became a microphone for Barbara, who slipped it out of my fingers and proceeded to announce, in the style of a game-show host, what we would be doing next. (Fieldnotes, September 12)

I found that imagination was everywhere: I saw it during observations at lunchtime and at recess; began to hear the ways it insinuated itself into periods when I or another teacher thought we were teaching and holding everyone's attention. I attempted to record any instances in which imagination showed itself through children's words or actions.

> At the end of the day, I ask the class, "What did you learn today?" Most state a fact, but Sophia says, "I learned to read" so emphatically that it seems as if it must have happened, which I know it didn't. Jamilla says, "I learned that when sunlight shines through brown hair, it turns white." I am surprised and ask her where she learned that. She says, "In music" and explains that the sunlight was shining through Sasha's hair in music and it looked white. The other children echo this, and it was clear that they had all noticed and wondered about it. (Fieldnotes, January 25)

Because I was extremely involved in surveying how imagination showed itself throughout the schoolday, I decided to observe the children at recess and lunchtime. They eventually realized that I was also interested in their outdoor play, so they readily showed me what they were doing. I found, as I did when I looked throughout the schoolday, that their play was often a drama encompassing elaborate fantasies. Further, few of the children ever chose to play alone, and as a result the recess dramas were collaborative constructions.

In March, for example, during a lunch recess Sophia began to talk to me and show me what she and her friends were doing way back in the bushes that bordered the play area. On March 15 she brought me what she called a "way finder," a twig with a piece of yellow wire wrapped around one end to make a handle and a loop twisted at the other end. I asked her what it was for and she replied, "Well, it's for finding your way when you're lost. You just give it a few shakes, then watch which way it points and go that way." And she gave it a few shakes and went off in the direction it was pointing. A few minutes later, Sasha, who had been playing with Sophia, ran up to me with a partially broken twig in the shape of an *H*, presented the twig to me saying it was "a puppet with two people," and ran back into the bushes.

Writing as Performance

Eventually the recess dramas spilled over into the classroom. I first spotted them in the context of "writing" that took the form of collaborative map-making. In early October, I recorded three boys making maps and discussing what they would be used for. The maps showed a lot of lines and X's and arrows. Tommy, who seemed to be directing the process, told me that it was a "war map" and that the war was a secret. The process was clearly a spontaneous prewriting activity that had begun on the playground at recess. The maps were made as props for the outside drama. They would be composed in the classroom at writing time and were taken outside to be used at lunch recess. Upon returning to the classroom in the afternoons, the boys would make more maps. During the process, each of the boys drew individual maps simultaneously. The following transcript illustrates the way in which the drama of planning for and carrying out their recess game was an integral part of the composing process.

> **BRIAN:** These three are gonna fight.
> **TOMMY:** We have to throw bombs. *(makes bombing noises)*
> **CHINUA:** Yeah, like acorns [meaning the acorns outside].
> **BRIAN:** I don't have a bomb.
> **TOMMY:** I have water balloons!
> **BRIAN:** Yeah!
> **ALL:** Water balloons!
> **CHINUA:** This is my map.

BRIAN: This is my map.

CHINUA: Look at my map.

(They look at each other's maps.)

BRIAN: That's a crazy map!

TOMMY: Look at this map!

BRIAN: What do you do there? *(pointing to a part of Tommy's map)*

TOMMY: *(following the line with his finger)* You go up here, go down, take a turn . . .

CHINUA: *(making beeping noises in the background as he draws dotted lines)*

TOMMY: We have to go all around here. *(drawing the path with a marker)*

CHINUA: Oh my god!

TOMMY: We have to get ready for Tony, for Sam, for Tony.

BRIAN: Are we gonna battle them?

ALL: Yeah!

BRIAN: Yeah!

TOMMY: I gave my plans to my friend. He's going to copy them out . . . Matt.

BRIAN: Matt?

TOMMY: He knows all about war.

BRIAN: I have, I have a cousin named Matt.

TOMMY: I'll bring in helmets from home.

CHINUA: I already got a helmet from home.

BRIAN: Me, too.

TOMMY: No, for when you go into *battle!* I'll bring you in some, tomorrow. I'll bring you in some weapons.

CHINUA: OK.

"Write That Picture"

The period of mapmaking was followed by more collaborations in which two boys or two girls would draw and write together. In the early part of the year, the story writing took the form of pictures for which they would dictate a text that I would write down.

Peter and Brian have been drawing collaborative picture stories for 3 days straight. They draw intensely, trading markers and using the same large piece of paper. The stories they tell, like the pictures, are dynamic, active, rich in detail. I take their dictation to get the stories down. As I write, the stories expand in new directions. *It feels like they are propelled by the fluidity of my pen moving on the page.* When I write, they watch closely and mouth the words with me. Their attention to the words is much greater than it would be if I weren't writing. (Fieldnotes, October 20)

I had deliberately decided early in the year that I wanted the children's writing to emerge naturally from within their imaginative process of story-making. So, instead of setting an expectation for the class that "writing" had to include words on a page, we talked instead about stories and the different forms they took. As the weeks passed, I did not press the children to write the words that went with the pictures they were drawing, although a few who were already early readers did so. Rather, I continued to take dictation, and gradually I started to think out loud as I wrote—sounding out the words they were dictating, noting *soto voce* when I needed a period or other punctuation mark.

Peter and Brian are still continuing their joint picture stories. The drawing at this point is everything. I'm not at all pushing the writing. I ask for only a few words in writing time, providing a model for them as they dictate longer texts and I write. (Fieldnotes, November 1)

Then came the day when Peter began to write his own stories. I was ecstatic, not only because he came to the process of writing on his own terms but also because the writing and the pictures were joined physically and imaginatively.

Peter writes his own picture story text! Very incoherent, but he spontaneously begins to write without asking for help. I was standing quite close as this happened. He was drawing a picture with a red marker, and when he finished drawing the ground at the bottom of the picture, there was no pause between the end of the picture and the beginning of his first words on a page. The marker just kept on going. (Fieldnotes, November 28)

As the year progressed and the children's writing skills improved, they would alternate the jobs of writing and drawing, as in the following collaboration, but they did not naturally separate the two processes in their minds. Further, as the following transcript shows, the stories were still being performed. In other words, the writers were simultaneously playing the parts of the characters in the stories, drawing the scenes, and writing the texts.

> **PETER:** *(to Brian)* Write that picture.
> **BRIAN:** Yeah, I'm writing it.
> **PETER:** OK. Pretend this is our car.
> **BRIAN:** OK. *(He draws the car.)* Pretend this is me. *(Brian draws himself.)*
> *(They turn the page to the next blank page.)*
> **PETER:** *(as if dictating the text)* Michael and Joe fell in the grave hole.
> **BRIAN:** Hey, what about me?
> **PETER:** You can't spell it.
> **BRIAN:** Yes, I can. *(He writes "JASN.")* Jason. Now read it.
> **PETER:** Michael and Jason fell in the grave hole.
>
> [Here I think Brian was playing the character of Jason in their story and Peter was Michael.]
>
> **BRIAN:** *(looking at the text)* Hey! It doesn't say "and Jason."
> **PETER:** It won't fit.
> **KAREN:** Yeah, it will, just put it there with my pen.
> **BRIAN:** *(uses the pen to write)* Now read it again. *(They read it together.)*
> **BRIAN:** Hey, I'm not in the picture. I'm going to write me in. *(He draws himself on that page.)*
> *(Later, as they are working on the picture:)*
> **BRIAN:** Hey, we don't have eyes. We can't see the ghost if we don't have eyes. I'll put them in.

This exchange was one I had seen before with these young writers; it is most probably one that other teachers of young children have also witnessed. *Writing* and *drawing* are used interchangeably. Also, *pretend* is inserted in their discourse as they draw the story out, literally drawing the story on the page, metaphorically pulling it out from their imagination and co-constructing a unified text. In most cases the writing process included appropriate noises and, sometimes, actions. Thus, I saw more clearly that for young writers performance and writing were intertwined as forms of expressions, and they arose from their social interactions.

FROM WRITING TO PLAYACTING TO PLAYWRITING

Often what we formally set out to accomplish with children is something they intuitively know how to do and will practice, if the environment permits. Predictably, as I directed the children's attention and mine toward the importance of performance, retellings, and oral expression, they responded by becoming deeply involved. In the afternoons, I began to audiotape and take fieldnotes on both the children's "free" drama sessions (meaning those I did not orchestrate) and those that I asked them to do for retellings of stories we'd read together. Their first dramatic attempts at both free drama and retellings were disorganized and incomplete, often consisting more of the preparation and use of props and costumes that I had provided in the drama area than the creation of texts, but the children didn't seem to mind or notice the "disorganization" that I saw. Every day a group would come forward to announce they had made a play. That would be a signal for the entire class to get a chair and drag it over to the drama center, where they would set up rows and wait expectantly for the performances to begin.

A typical performance in early October included five children and one of our pet cockatiels as players. The play began in school; then everyone became fairies at Ellie's suggestion; then they were tin men at Barbara's suggestion; then they "transformed" into pumpkins and a farmer. "Part Two: Now we switch parts" was announced and new parts sprang from nothing. "Now we are warriors on a ship." Beyond that minimalistic kind of narration, the play proceeded without words to accompany the actors' actions.

The Role of Critique

> By gradually eliminating whatever proved superfluous, we found that theater can exist without make-up, without autonomic costume and scenography, without a separate performance area ... without lighting and sound effects. It cannot exist without the actor-spectator relationship of perceptual, direct, "live communion." (Grotowski, 1968, p. 19)

Throughout the year, the children's performances developed in response to constant feedback and interaction with the audience as a group and myself as a kind of consultant as well as with their growing familiarity with performance as a way to process new texts. As Grotowski points out, their understanding of what became important for performances developed because of the "actor-spectator relationship of perceptual, direct, 'live communion.'"

Early in the year I insisted that each performance be followed by a response period from the audience, and I modeled how to respond to a play as a spectator. My commitment to having a period of response following performances was based on Elwyn Richardson's (1964) concept of "valuing" in which critique of an artwork, a piece of writing, or a performance develops from a collectively established set of values of what is aesthetically pleasing for the audience. In *In the Early World,* Richardson (1964) describes his work as a teacher in a rural, multiage classroom. The evolution of the concept of valuing developed as he and his students became involved in a multiarts curriculum.

> All work was presented in some way or other to the whole class, and a basis of values was developed, so that through the process of discussion and assessment a piece of prose or poetry was recognized as being of value or not. (Richardson, 1964, p. 36)

In the process of valuing, small and large gains are recognized and affirmed in different ways, and the process is always done collaboratively.

What Is a Performance?

While there has been a great deal of research and writing about responding to writing with a class, in this case our focus was on developing performance texts. We slowly began to define a small set of criteria about what made one performance more satisfying than another, what Richardson (1964) calls "recognition of small excellences" (p. 112).

When the year began, I paid close attention to the ways in which the children were expressing their understanding of what a performance was. After working with Denzel (see Chapter 1), I was, of course, interested in having them make a *connection between their imaginative ideas as they were embodied in their performances and the creation of an accompanying oral text or narrative.* Thus, when I began to interact with the children as they made their plays, the values I was encouraging through my critique were based on the desire for that connection. I wanted their words.

Why Words? The reader will recall from Chapter 1 my struggle to engage Denzel with the stories in books. He did not naturally see stories as occurring in the words and pictures of the storybook. Rather, for Denzel stories were oral, told by a person to a group of peers. In other words, in the silence that surrounded the reading of a story, when other children were attaching image and thought to the words and pictures in the text, Denzel was not. That position, in turn, affected his comprehension of, and attention to, many of the texts we read as part of our studies, preventing him from taking full advantage of them as resources for his own learning.

Therefore, although I knew that silence was an important part of all artistic activity, I had learned from Denzel that I wanted children's words for two reasons: First, I knew from my work with Science Talks (Gallas, 1995) that pairing ideas, images, and actions with words furthered the development and elaboration of my students' ideas and thought processes. Second, though artistic works are often conceived in silence, in most cases they are viewed by an audience, and that viewing provokes a response that takes the form of language, spoken and written. As Grumet (1988), Grotowski (1968), and Richardson (1964) all point out, serious artistic work is at different points presented to an audience for critique, valuing, and communion. Thus, the artist begins a conversation that invites the audience to join in. I wanted all my students to be fully engaged in those conversations. Hence, I wanted their words. (See Chapter 6 for more on the role of the audience in developing literate behaviors.)

For some of the boys in my first-grade class, though, drama meant battles filled with pretend fights, grunts, and the noises of weapons, but no words. When I saw this trend, I immediately intervened, asking not that the battles cease, as I would have in the past, but rather that they include words.

> Sonny and Peter—third day in a row in drama. It becomes a big fight: lots of sounds but little language. Lots of running, jumping, and falling, but no extension of language. They seem locked in the physical. Finally, after 30 minutes, I go in and make a new rule: "No fighting in a play without using words." Sonny is furious and stomps out and over to the block area, where they start again. This time I walk quite slowly by them and they quietly continue the battle. I sit down right next to them and Peter says, "We can fight like that here, right?"
>   "No," I say, "not here either."
>   "Where?" Peter says.

"At home," I answer.

Sonny stomps off again. Peter follows. I walk over to the big steps and sit down. Soon Sonny returns, not scowling any longer. Peter comes up the steps and sees Brian and Nat playing Legos and says, "Where's that teacher? I'm going to ask her something." He finds me and points at them as they move their Legos across the steps. He says, "They're fighting."

"How can you tell?" I ask.

"I heard them."

"Let's listen," I say. He is quiet. We hear the boys pretending there will be battles and talking as if they are in a battle. Behind me Peter starts to make soft, shooting sounds.

"See," he says, grinning.

"Peter," I say, "that's you."

"No," he says, "they're really fighting!" (Fieldnotes, September 14)

From that exchange came a discussion of what the difference was that I was looking for. I had to explain to Peter and Sonny the difference between a rough-and-tumble, silent battle in the drama center and a battle with Legos that included words. Thus began the first steps toward establishing the values that would be the underpinning of all our future critiques and exchanges around their performances. However, I think it's important to state here that those values were not in the end defined totally from my perspective. Early in the year I thought I knew what had to happen: I wanted the silent imaginative dramas to have a spoken story attached to them. But, beginning with that first exchange with Peter and Sonny, I had to consider, once again, why my ideas should take precedence. Peter's comment, "No, they're really fighting," signaled that the distinctions among a silent pretend fight, a real-life fight, and a drama or a story were subtle, and he, for one, wasn't ready to accept my opinion on it without debate.

Creating Scripts. In the first part of the year, learning about how words fit into the process of creating a performance took place with the small groups of actors and myself, as they worked in the drama center. As an example, the following fieldnotes show how even a short interaction with me around the content of the play would immediately transform it, causing the language and action to be more complex.

> Donaldo, Tommy, Sophia, Jamilla, and Yasuka are playing doctor. Very
> little plot, just a lot of shots being given. I go into the group, sit with
> Dr. Sophia, and do a little coaching, prompting them to tell what
> they're doing and asking them questions about the play. I leave.
> (Fieldnotes, November 13, 1:00)

> I return to the doctors. They have a "911" scenario going. Tommy is
> unconscious in a burning house. The children have become para-
> medics and there is much more talk. Donaldo is using expressive terms
> as part of the action, like, "Look! The fire!" They run back and forth.
> The action, props, and costumes spread out into the meeting area.
> The action is fierce. (Fieldnotes, November 13, 1:30)

As the fall progressed, we began having brief discussions at the end of
the plays about what the audience—including myself or my intern, Sarah—
thought. By November, I had also introduced the process of retellings of
stories as a resource for playmaking, and some children took up this strategy as a vehicle for their plays. That, in turn, increased their use of language
as an embellishment of the action. When the audience viewed those kinds
of plays, they would object if a particular part weren't accompanied by an
appropriate text. On any given afternoon, moreover, as many as three different groups would be working on a play. For example, on November 8,
three plays occurred. In the first, a few children did a retelling of *The Biggest
Pumpkin Ever* (Kroll, 1984).

> Ellie, the narrator, is dressed in a clown suit and is orchestrating the
> play by giving directions to the actors. Sasha has covered herself with
> fluorescent Mylar and is the pumpkin. Sophia, wearing a crown, is also
> growing a second pumpkin. That's about it.

The second play was titled, "A Rock and Roll Band."

> Nat, Brian, Boris, Tommy, and Danny have built instruments in the block
> area. They start "playing" an old surfing song. "Let's go surfing now" . . .
> ?? They stop. Then they decide to play another. Barbara says, "Tommy,
> you have to face the audience." [This is a new learning since Septem-
> ber. It happened after we critiqued an earlier version of their act. The
> class decided that when you sang, you needed to face your audience.]

The third play was a second performance of *The Biggest Pumpkin Ever.*

> Ellie is very true to the story. Jamilla improvises and is less intelligi-
> ble. Ellie signals a time change, "the next day." [This is new, the
> announcement of a time change, based on our critique of their
> first version.] Everything is a prop (hanger, mirror). The children
> dress up just for the effect of wearing a costume, even if it is totally
> unrelated to their plot. Finally, Sasha, the pumpkin, says, "Well,
> that's it."

By February our work with retellings had had a great effect on the language used to accompany the action. For example, we spent part of February reading different versions of the folktale "The Magic Fish." On one
afternoon I asked the children to form themselves into groups of three and
develop a performance of the story. Following each performance, we talked
about their work, and in some cases the audience sent them back to revise
the piece. My fieldnotes record two notable instances when children surprised me or others with their work. First, Emily, whom we met in the Introduction and will revisit in Chapter 4, was uncharacteristically dynamic.
Normally soft spoken and retiring, she spoke loudly and clearly as the fisherman's wife, looking straight out at the audience and reciting her part ver-
batim from the text with great presence. As the reader may recall, upon
entering first grade Emily was a child who was not terribly interested in
fiction texts because they weren't true, but by March a shift had taken
place that enabled her to take a major role in the retelling of a text and do
it convincingly.

In a contrasting way, Sophia's rendition of the character of the fisherman's wife offered evidence of another outcome of continuous work with
performance. In her group's performance, Sophia stopped the action mid-
way, turned to me, and said, "Can I change the story?" I indicated that she
could, and she proceeded to change the dialogue between the fisherman and
his wife that had been repeated in so many written versions of the story.
When the fisherman asked her what she wanted, instead of saying she
wanted "the sun, the moon, and the stars" as the texts all said, she said, "I
want a pizza store, a McDonald's, and all the money in the world," which
evoked a strong positive reaction from her audience. Here again, as in so
many areas of our classroom life, Sophia's active work with her imagination changed a basic value about dramatic renderings of literature that was

later taken up by other children in the class—that stories can be changed by performers to suit their purposes.

Collaboration

> **SOPHIA:** Karen, Barbara and I have our favorite word, but is it a swear?
>
> **KAREN:** What is it?
>
> **SOPHIA:** *Dead person.*
>
> **KAREN:** *(laughing)* No, it's not a swear.
>
> **SOPHIA:** Good, 'cause we really like to say it. (Fieldnotes, May 2)

> The most desirable situation . . . is that which the child himself creates. . . . The children have to begin from something genuine and personal and come to realize it more fully or exactly during the expression. (Richardson, 1964, pp. 117–118)

Sophia and Barbara's short conversation with me illustrates the kind of climate that had emerged in the classroom. They came to me with what they considered to be a "loaded" question—something that might possibly be inappropriate to present to a teacher. Their performances in class frequently depended on an aura of risk and surprise that they created through their choice of topic and the way they played with nuances of language. By bringing their question to me, they were accomplishing two things: First, they were clarifying that the phrase *dead person* was socially acceptable. Second, they were testing their material on me to see its effect. Their actions speak to Richardson's observation that children's artistic efforts gain depth when they originate with the child and are extended through their interactions with adults and each other.

In the class as a whole, I found that the children who regularly worked with drama during the week soon formed small repertory groups, preferring to develop plays with a consistent cohort who shared their interests in particular themes. Each cohort had a different flavor to its plays and became increasingly more sophisticated in its productions as the children moved deeper into their preferred themes and responded to contact with their audience. For example, Boris, Peter, Brian, Sonny, and Tommy regularly enacted "battles" or other more physical narratives, while Nat, Sasha, Sophia, Jamilla,

Barbara, Ellie, and Julie preferred more literary narratives. In mid-March I recorded the following drama from a small group of the literary players in my field notes:

> **NAT:** *(announces the play)* "Grammy and Darla."
> **JULIE:** Grammy, please can you tell me a story?
> **SASHA:** OK. This is dedicated to Samantha, my ancestor, who lived over a thousand years ago.
>
> [This is an elaborate rehearsal of an evolving play, very conceptual. There is Nat, who plays the announcer and a voice in the background called the "time passer." Julie and Sasha are granddaughter and grand-mom, and Sasha is telling the story to Julie. Barbara has two dolls who act out the story as it is told.]
>
> **NAT:** *(as a voice in the background)* And the time passes.
> **SASHA:** *(to Julie)* Do you remember the time when you were a baby and I was 71? *(an aside to the audience)* I am really old!
> **NAT:** *(voice in the background)* How old are you?
> **SASHA:** I'm . . .
> **NAT:** You should live to be 121.
> **SASHA:** OK. I'm 100 now . . . I remember the time when I rocked you in the little blanket in a little pail. Do you remember when you would fit in this blanket? *(pauses, then begins in a new wistful tone)* Once upon in the night of the moon, once you slept, and once, one more time, you ate spaghetti and your face got smothered in tomato sauce. And I remember the time tomato sauce got up your nose.
> **NAT:** Dinner's ready.

This text offers the flavor that the children's literary work had taken on. They were both poetic and funny, filled with improvisations based on the responses they were getting from their own co-actors and the audience. They also created different kinds of roles so that all actors could participate. In this case, although there were only two characters, Grammy and Darla, by making Nat a narrator and adding in the dolls, which Barbara used as puppets, each player could be in the play.

In the same week, I observed the boys who preferred action plays perform the following piece. In this case, we can see how the value of embellishing action with words had seeped into the narratives. Tommy, Brian, Sonny, and

Peter had discovered some armor that Sophia had brought into the drama corner from home. Tommy and Brian had swords and shields and, as the play opened, they were battling it out. Sonny had a large toy clock and was acting as a timekeeper for the fight. I sat down to watch and said, as I often did, "Any words?" Peter heard me and said to the actors, "Guys, some words." They looked over at him and began to talk as they fought. Peter said, "More words." Then the actors traded places and Tommy became the timekeeper.

> **TOMMY:** It's 12:00 in the morning. Now they're going to fight until midnight.
> **PETER:** You will never destroy me again.
> **SONNY:** Yes, I will.
> **PETER:** And my mom will come to defeat you!
> **SONNY:** You will never defeat me!
> *(They fight with a lot of "bshtts" and "ooh's.")*
> **TOMMY:** Stop ducking! You cannot duck! Ready, go! The fight has begun!

The actors traded insults about whose magic was best. Note, here, how Tommy acted as the narrator, and both he and Peter played the part of the director of the action.

Toward the end of the year, the literary players added a new element to some of their performances: opera.

> Sophia, Barbara, and Sasha are having a play about a grandmother, granddaughter, and her cat. The grandmother tells a story of a cat who falls into a magic pool, then comes out, and is magic. They are negotiating the narrative. Sophia wants the story only to be about the magic cat. Sasha wants a storyteller to tell the story while they act it out. Finally they agree when Sophia says, "Include my part with your part, but don't change my part." Sophia is wearing cat's ears. Sasha has a ragged piece of cloth on her head for a scarf. She is old and poor (as she often is in their plays). I walk away to see another child's block building and then return. Sophia is dressing Barbara in a beautiful black dress. Sasha is sleeping peacefully on two adjoined chairs. She is covered by a piece of orange Mylar.
>
> Sophia dresses Barbara and sings to her lovingly, "Now you are so beautiful. Put on this beautiful dress. Stay here with me. . . ."
>
> [This is the first time I've heard singing in our class plays as a form of operatic text.] (Fieldnotes, April 8)

IMAGINATION AS A SUBTEXT

PETER: If I'm in the bathroom and I think bad things are in the dark,
I just flush the toilet and run out.

JAMILLA: Me, too. Sometimes in the girls' bathroom, I get scared and
I just flush the toilet and run out. I don't even wash my hands.

PETER: And once, me, Brian, and Sonny were in the art area, and we
were planning something, and we scared ourselves. We had to leave
that place and come up here. (Fieldnotes, Math, March 28)

Anne Hass Dyson (1993) has talked about official and unofficial worlds
of children's experience in school, the official being scripts and activities that
are sanctioned by the teacher and the school, and the unofficial being those
that occur among children outside the provenance of the teacher. In my
book on power, identity, and gender (Gallas, 1998), I proposed that the
unofficial agendas of children ought to be seen as a subtextual dynamic that
permeates classroom activity and influences all aspects of teaching and
learning, and that it is critical that teachers recognize those agendas and
bring them into the official business of the classroom.

Earlier in this book I described how I began with a study of my personal
imaginative life (see Chapter 2) only to find that there was no area of my
life that was not affected by my imagination. After looking at the work of
this class of first graders and working with subsequent classes, it is clear to
me that the imagination of my students is constantly operating (both indi-
vidually and collectively) under the surface of daily life as a subtextual phenomenon; and as it works, it powerfully influences a student's and a classroom community's actions as learners.

The excerpt above about being afraid took place in a time following
math instruction when the children worked in pairs or trios with math
games. It indicates to me not that Peter and Jamilla were not thinking about
math, but rather that in the process of playing the game, moving the pieces,
and counting the dots on the dice, they had started an important conversation about being afraid, a conversation made possible by the sociability
of the game format and, possibly, by the process of playing. Some observers
might say those children were off-task and therefore wouldn't receive the
full benefit of the activity, but what this observation shows me is the way
in which our imaginations are constantly moving in and out of our daily
activities. Even when children appear to be quiet and focused on our agen-

das as teachers, they may also be working on other imaginative things, just as we would be doing in the same circumstances: remembering the past, pondering the future, wondering about the way light is passing through hair, frightening ourselves as we remember footsteps behind us on a dark stair or a spider lurking in a bathroom sink.

SOPHIA: Karen, I'm going to tell you a secret.
KAREN: What?
SOPHIA: *(whispers in my ear)* I'm going deep in the ocean to find a treasure.
KAREN: When?
SOPHIA: Tomorrow. I'm so excited!

PART II

Building a Literate Identity

"The House Was Quiet and the World Was Calm"

by Wallace Stevens

The house was quiet and the world was calm.
The reader became the book; and summer night

Was like the conscious being of the book.
The house was quiet and the world was calm.

The words were spoken as if there was no book,
Except that the reader leaned above the page,

Wanted to lean, wanted much most to be
The Scholar to whom his book is true, to whom

The summer night is like a perfection of thought.
The house was quiet because it had to be.

The quiet was part of the meaning, part of the mind:
The access of perfection to the page.

And the whole world was calm. The truth in a calm world
In which there is no other meaning, itself

Is calm, itself is summer and night, itself
Is the reader leaning late and reading there.

When I first encountered this poem, it held for me a complete and integrated picture of an individual striving to become a reader and a scholar. There was, first, the reader's desire to fall into the book and be lost in it, a desire formed, in part, from having seen and admired another skilled reader at work. Then, I saw the conditions under which that kind of deep involvement occurred: the quiet of the summer night as "part of the meaning, part of the mind"—a liminal space in which imagination could soar. The desire to be a scholar and the access to "truth" that role might provide is realized when the reader's desire—the setting of summer and night—and the text fuse in the moment of reading. But, of course, the poem itself does not parse out those requirements. It cloaks them in metaphor and imagery, and that cloaking, itself an imaginative exercise, forced me to see the "whole" of literacy and imagination. The reading transforms the reader, the night, summer, and the meaning of the text itself. Thus, while I can take apart this poem to see what each section signified for me as a reader, I cannot express the wholeness of the poem better than the poem itself expresses it.

In the chapters that follow, I take apart what I have found out about imagination and its relationship to literacy to make them more visible. But, like the poem above, the action of imagination in that process of becoming educated is, in reality, "cloaked" and obscured from view. My parsing of the process is a device to draw attention to different aspects of imagination at work. It represents some of the pieces, not the whole.

CHAPTER 4

Talking to Ants:
Imagination and Identity

Emily is sharing a toy preying mantis. In answer to a question asking how she knows what it is, she says, "Well, I can just tell by looking at them what they are and I know how to talk to them." She (the preying mantis) said she had already laid her egg case. Then Emily tells how "when I go out to the garden with my dad, I just put my little toy animals on a string, and then go out so they can't get away." Later, at story time, I glance over at Emily and she has the fake preying mantis sitting on top of her head as she listens. (Fieldnotes, December 19)

Because our first-grade class had the regular forum of sharing time within which the children could present themselves and their interests to their friends, we gradually learned more and more about Emily's remarkable identification with the world of insects. At the same time, as she became more comfortable with that forum, Emily used it to fully define herself as a budding entomologist, and she enabled me to observe how that process was dependent on the active work of her imagination. Later in the year, she began to make friends with the other children, and most often the context of their play revolved around Emily's fascination with insects. Thus, her devotion to the subject pulled other children into it so that eventually she had collaborators in her insect hunts and her dramatic play.

This morning Emily and Sasha are sitting, drawing in their art journals. As I stop by, I ask Emily what she's drawing.

EMILY: It's me being a bug.
SASHA: Yeah, yesterday when we played we were being magic bugs. It was really fun.

EMILY: And we could change anytime. So we could be a cockroach, then an ant, then a bee and sting anyone. (Fieldnotes, January 30)

CONNECTING OBSERVATION WITH THEORY

As a teacher-researcher seeking to find guidance in making imagination logical, or at least tangible to myself and others, I have been drawn to theoretical positions that acknowledge the highly individual, organic nature of identifying with a subject and that also emphasize that that identification needs a social context to fully develop. Four approaches to literacy helped me clarify what I was seeing in my data.

Sylvia Ashton-Warner: Tapping Creativity

Ashton-Warner (1963), in her seminal work on the teaching of reading, described her discovery that to be successful with Maori children, she had to exploit what she called the "volcanic vent" of the child, the child's inner source of creativity and violence (p. 29). Ashton-Warner's conviction gave rise to her articulation of what she called the organic reading method and the use of key vocabulary for teaching reading and writing. For Ashton-Warner, literacy was achieved by tapping into the center of her students' inner life and using their hopes, fears, fantasies, and conflicts to make words and the act of reading *essential.* As she writes:

> I see the mind of the five year old as a volcano with two vents: destructiveness and creativeness. . . . And it seems to me that since these words of the key vocabulary are no less than the captions of the dynamic life itself, they course out through the creative channel. . . . First words must mean something to a child. First words must have intense meaning for a child. They must be part of his being. . . . Pleasant words won't do. Respectable words won't do. They must be words organically tied, organically born from the dynamic life itself. They must be words that are already part of the child's being. (p. 30)

Of course, just as it did in the 1960s when *Teacher* was first published, Ashton-Warner's theory of reading flies in the face of the functional reading programs that are once again gaining currency in schools. At the time, she agonized over how her pedagogical beliefs made her an outsider in her field:

> We had our grading this week. The men were well marked . . . but as usual I was very low. There's no doubt about it. I am a very low-ability teacher . . . maybe it is a distinction of some kind to be unacceptable in New Zealand teaching. (p. 117)

Yet she remained convinced, through her classroom research, that the organic method helped her Maori students master the "idea" of reading.

Ashton-Warner's identification of "the dynamic life" of the child moves me closer to defining the process I am seeking to understand. In considering her position, I see a commitment to the primacy of imagination as a vehicle for building a literate identity. Note, here, that the creative process produces words that are "the captions of the dynamic life," but as a teacher, it is the center of the child's being she is after. To illustrate how she draws upon that center, Ashton-Warner provides a description of the methods of her practice. Rich experiences were offered in all of the arts, each one intended to further what she called the alternating processes of "intake" and "output," or "breathe in" and "breathe out" (p. 89). In other words, the first part of each day explicitly introduced the world of language and literacy to her students, while the next part called on them to make meaning of that world through expressive action. In addition, Ashton-Warner recognized the essential role that social and cultural factors played in literacy learning, complaining at one point,

> From long sitting, watching, pondering (all so unprofessional) I have found the worst enemies to what we call teaching. . . . The first is the children's interest in each other. It plays the very devil with orthodox method. . . . In self-defense I've got to use the damn thing. (p. 103)

Thus, the teaching of reading was tied both to the inner world of the child and to the outer world of the classroom where relationships powerfully influenced learning.

James Gee: Mastering a Discourse

From a different tradition, Gee (1996) has described literacy as being a process that requires a student to master more than language use. He places the achievement of literacy in the realm of mastery of a discourse. To do that, a student must step into the shoes, for example, of a mathematician:

He or she must walk, talk, live, eat, and breathe mathematics. True literacy, therefore, is achieved when an individual begins to live in the body of a subject, identifying with it in a visceral, organic way and translating that identification into action in the world. It requires both mastery of the subject itself and a public presentation of self as expert: One must both believe and know, and one must also convince others.

> Discourses are ways of being in the world, or forms of life which integrate words, acts, values, beliefs, attitudes, and social identities, as well as gestures, glances, body positions, and clothes. A Discourse is a sort of identity kit which comes complete with the appropriate costume and instructions on how to act, talk, and often write, so as to take on a particular social role that others will recognize. (Gee, 1996, p. 127)

Here, again, we can recall Emily's intense involvement with her subject and the beginnings of her public presentation of self as an expert within the classroom. This framework for literacy, like Ashton-Warner's, melds the inner and outer worlds of the student in what might be called an "inside-out" process.

Madeline Grumet: Bodyreading

Grumet (1988), in proposing a theory of "bodyreading," bridges the positions of Ashton-Warner as teacher-researcher and Gee as sociolinguist. Grumet looks deeply into the meaning of reading as a broad cultural practice embedded in the particularities of each individual's social, physical, and emotional life—a practice that she believes has been cut out of the process of schooling. She proposes that learning to read in our schools requires children to move from the physical world of body, movement, and touch into a detached and decontextualized world of words where The Look must repudiate touch and imagination becomes localized in The Look (p. 107).

It is important to note here that when I encountered Denzel, I believed the achievement of The Look was the appropriate goal of story time. (See Chapter 1.) This is, I think, what I saw in my other students and wanted to teach to Denzel. Yet in her conceptualization of the disconnect between the individual child and the school, Grumet (1988) strives, as do Ashton-Warner and Gee, to relocate the center of learning organically in the idea of bodyreading:

> In "bodyreading" I borrow this body-subject to run some errands, to bring what we know to where we live, to bring reading home again. To bring what we know to where we live has not always been the project of curriculum, for schooling . . . has functioned to repudiate the body, the place where it lives, and the people who care for it. (p. 129)

Here Grumet clarifies the importance of identity as originating in the context of the learner's world, drawing attention to the interaction between the dynamic inner life of the individual and the life of home and school. She uses the image of reading as living in the body to convey the sense that reading is not a process that takes place above the neck, but is rather an all-encompassing mind–body activity.

Lave and Wenger: Learning Involves the Whole Person

Finally, Lave and Wenger (1991), in defining what they call "legitimate peripheral participation," point me toward an understanding of how I, as a teacher, am included in the process of mind–body–world integration that Ashton-Warner, Gee, and Grumet propose.

> As an aspect of social practice, learning involves the whole person: it implies not only a relation to specific activities, but a relation to social communities—it implies becoming a full participant, a member, a kind of person. (Lave & Wenger, 1991, p. 53)

Lave and Wenger explore the process of apprenticeship as a potential model for literacy instruction, describing how apprentice learners are gradually introduced to important literate practices through "legitimate access," that is, through real-life involvement in those practices in the company of more experienced practitioners, such as teachers.

BUILDING AN INSIDE-OUT THEORY OF LITERACY LEARNING

From these four conceptual positions, I want to propose a framework that links my questions about imagination with what I am calling an inside-out theory of literacy learning. In doing so, I will locate the development of children's identities as learners within the interaction between self and world. I will also describe what entering a discourse through the imagination looks like as well as how that entry becomes public so that I can participate in it and further my students' engagement with literate practices. In my mind, the positions of Ashton-Warner, Gee, Grumet, and Lave and Wenger all speak to the centrality of imagination in literacy learning. The data that follow enable us to see that process as one that integrates mind, body, head, heart, and world. It will also reveal my sometimes clumsy discovery of the ways in which my students naturally expressed that integration.

Walking the Walk and Talking the Talk

In my inquiry into imagination, I hoped to describe the formation of identity *through* imagination within the social context of my classrooms. I wanted to understand how children's social interactions and symbolic contacts with the materials, processes, and symbol systems of instruction within a subject did or did not evolve into a personal identification with that subject—that is, into a belief that the subject was one they could master or be good at. Cobb (1993) proposes that

> as the child develops a continually wider ability to create ever greater complexity of gestalten in play, thought, and word, the shape and meaning of his perceptual world emerges, and the continual interplay of perceptual relations with environment sharpens the contours of his own image and deepens the reflections of the effects of his own identity on others. (p. 95)

The following fieldnotes record an interaction I had with Sabrina (whom we will meet again in Chapters 5 and 6) around her belief that she was not a competent artist. This event took place in her kindergarten year.

> Sketching exercise this week was to sketch an insect from a picture in a book. Sabrina chose an ant and rendered it accurately, including the minute hairs on the legs. It was quite impressive. Then today, at morning journal time when she went to work, drawing yet again the same picture she's drawn since September of two dogs and two people, the dogs in black, the people like cartoons, I asked her to plan for a new kind of picture. She said to me in her characteristically engaging and questioning voice, "But what should I draw?"

> We discussed some possibilities and decided upon a flower, and she
> said, brightly and without any tension, "But I don't know how to draw
> flowers."
>   I said, "Have you tried?" and she responded, "No, I haven't. Will
> you help me?" I agreed and we talked through the components of
> a flower and the colors she might need. I walked away thinking she
> would need more help from me, but then, about 10 minutes later,
> she walked up to me smiling broadly and presented me with a picture
> of two flowers in a garden and an exuberant Sabrina standing next to
> them. (Fieldnotes, October 24)

In this short interaction with me, Sabrina had broken through the standard
picture she'd been doing for 2 months and come out with a remarkable
drawing. I knew she was capable of doing this kind of work from observing her, but she had not realized this herself. The moment of producing the
flower picture represented the beginning of her awareness that she had the
ability to draw complex pictures, and it occurred because she was gradually
prompted through her interactions with me to, as Cobb put it, "create ever
greater complexity of gestalten in play, thought, and word." In that process
of being prodded to look outward and break away from her repetitive representation of her family, Sabrina began to redefine herself as an artist who
was passionately engaged with drawing, painting, and decoration.

In a similar way, because I work with young children, I have recorded
many different occasions when the world of print and numbers first become
part of a young child's psyche. For example, my fieldnotes from 1998 record
George (whom we will also meet again in Chapter 6) as he began to make
contact with math and writing. George was a child who might normally be
termed "developmentally delayed." He was socially and academically imma-
ture and had some speech and language problems. Adjusting to the rou-
tines and instructional agendas of kindergarten was quite difficult for him,
but he very much wanted to participate in our activities. What follows are
my observations of George in November as he began to participate in our
instructional activities.

> George! The rush of small steps is way too fast for me to ever cover
> entirely. *Math exercise:* I say to the class, "I'm thinking of a number
> between 1 and 9." (The number I'm thinking of is 5.) I write on the
> board: 1 ◄——► 9 as a mnemonic for them to work with. A child
> guesses "6." I don't respond positively or negatively; instead I write

←――――― 6, which they know by now means "it is less than 6". The next child guesses "1." I write 1 ―――――▶. The next guess is "2." I write 2 ―――――▶. George raises his hand and says "5." I am astonished. The class is astonished. George is exultant. Two of the children nearest him grab him and give him a huge bear hug. The whole class cheers and claps. George practically levitates.

OK, I think, a lucky guess. Two days later, same thing: He gets it again. The children exult. He has something, this understanding about numbers, arrows, and the use of symbols.

The graphs: Two graphs ago, as we were reviewing our graph of "our favorite ice cream flavors," George came up to the front of the group and said, "I want to count" (something he used to weep over early in the year when he realized he didn't know how to count), and he counted each row. When I asked for a volunteer to "read" our graph and summarize what we found out, George volunteered. Now he does it routinely, counting as high as 12 on our latest "hair color" graph. He can't recognize the numeral 12, but he can count to it.

Writing: Last Thursday, George drew a picture in his journal; wrote, very focused, all kinds of scribbles, about 28 lines or so of them. He said to me, "What does it say?" I said, "Well, can you read it to me?" He does, following his print meticulously with his finger, then coming to the end of a line with more words coming out of his mouth, and he says, "No, wait. That not there." He writes ferociously above the print that is already there, adding more lines and squiggles, then rereads, following the same track as the first time and moving up to the top row for the part he thought of later. Moving up exactly to the right place where the forgotten words were written. (Fieldnotes, November 1998)

What these notes about George present for us is a glimpse into how an inside-out theory of literacy learning might look in one child's life. Here we see the melding of Ashton-Warner's theory that literacy begins with the "captions of the dynamic life of the child" (1963, p. 30) with Grumet's belief that learning begins with an integration of body and mind. Writing, for George, surfaces through the "creative vent," but it is realized in the movement of his hand across the page. These moments represented the beginning of one child's belief that he is a mathematician and he is a writer. They show the early stages of building an "identity kit" (Gee, 1996) as a literate individual. George's perception of himself is changing and expanding as he comes in contact with new ways of thinking about the world and new symbol systems. The growth of his identity is fueled by his realization that he is "getting" it—that what was once strange and foreign is beginning to make sense—and by the celebration of his achievements with his classmates and myself.

This observation is also rich with different elements of the workings of imagination. The ability to view an arrow as an indicator of relative value requires an imaginative leap. The ability to "read" the symbolic representations on a picture graph as information requires a decontextualization of the process of eating ice cream—another imaginative leap. The desire to write lines of squiggles and curves, and then to read them out loud with the knowledge that they represent the words you were thinking as you wrote, is both a leap toward symbolization and the beginning of a belief that you are a writer with important things to say.

Imagination and Reading

> Consider the following: alone in the midst of grownups, I was a miniature adult and read books written for adults. That already sounds false, since, at the same time, I remained a child. I am claiming that I was guilty.... The fact remains that my hunting and exploration were part of the family play-acting, that the grown-ups were delighted by it, and that I knew it.... How could I determine—especially after so many years—the imperceptible and shifting frontier that separates possession from hamming? I would lie on my stomach, facing the windows, with an open book in front of me, a glass of wine-tinted water at my right, and a slice of bread and jam on a plate at my left. Even in solitude I was putting on an act. (Sartre, 1964, pp. 43–44)

In this excerpt from his memoir, Sartre presents a memory of himself as an early reader. He is reading, but he is also involved in a performance. His audience is the adults in his family, and his goal is to please and impress them. His identity as a reader is embedded in family life; it is a full and complex identity, one that many of us have experienced ourselves and observed in our own children. Yet I know from my work with Denzel that, for some children, the process of identification with a subject is sparse and dispassionate. Denzel could learn to read the words on the page of a book, but he did not feel the imaginative and personal pull of those words. The words on the pages were sounds to be decoded. They did not excite him. Math was meant to be rows of numbers that one would add and subtract; they were not a source of curiosity or information about his life. As Denzel's teacher, I could not demand the kind of engagement that Sartre describes and that I had seen in George, because that rupture in his identification with reading or math occurred *before he even made an approach to the texts* we were studying—at times before the book was even opened! (See Chapter 8 for more on "approach.")

It is only logical to assume that Denzel's perceptual world, his understanding of what it meant to be a reader or a mathematician, was, as with any other child, being powerfully influenced by a personal cultural space beyond the domain of my classroom. As Lave and Wenger (1991) point out:

> Activities, tasks, functions and understandings do not exist in isolation; they are part of broader social systems of relations in which they have meaning. . . . The person is defined by as well as defines these relations. Learning thus implies becoming a different person with respect to the possibilities enabled by these systems of relations. To ignore this aspect of learning is to overlook the fact that learning involves the construction of identities. (p. 53)

Lave and Wenger emphasize here the active role of the individual in "defining" the meaning of learning activities. That definition occurs both in and outside school. And while they stress that learning "involves the construction of identities," that process is a highly individual and indeterminate process.

As a teacher, therefore, it was crucial that my understanding of the relationship of identity to this process of "becoming" be expanded. I believe that when the student's preconceptions, the texts being studied, and the instructional goals of the teacher come in contact, they are processed through the lens of this personal, cultural space. *As a teacher, I must examine and describe that space in order to bring learning home to where it lives.* As I studied imagination, I began to ask myself this question: When imagination is being used in the service of developing an identity as a scientist, a mathematician, a reader, a writer, how does that look? Where does deep personal contact with a subject begin?

The Scientific Imagination

Typically, I came across a part of the answer in the following manner. During a visit to the SciTechatorium, the hands-on science museum located on the campus of the charter school where I was teaching a kindergarten class, I observed two of my kindergarten boys during our weekly visits. Over a 3-week period, they spent their time developing an elaborate fantasy around a large telescope in an astronomy exhibit. The exhibit itself included models of the space shuttle, a tile from one of the shuttles, posters of planets and the different shuttles and the sun, a timeline of space exploration, and so on. On one particular day, the two boys started to extend their fantasy to all parts of the museum and were running around as if chasing aliens. I approached them to curb this behavior, acting intuitively on the assumption that pretending is hazardous in a place full of precious exhibits. In the midst of my intervention, I stopped, realizing the absurdity of what I was saying, given my commitment to the place of wonder and imagination in the scientific process. I apologized for having interrupted and urged them to continue with their play but to limit their movement around the museum. They happily agreed and continued on while I ran to get pencil and paper to take down their talk. As I did so, I looked around and observed that every single child in my class was doing the same thing all over the museum. Some were more public about their fantasies, some completely silent, but all seemed to be building imaginary worlds using the exhibits in the museum as the catalysts, and most, in an incipient way, were assuming the role of the scientist in their explorations of those worlds.

Here is a transcript from four children working in a fossils exhibit. They were using small brushes to uncover molds of fossil remains covered with sand. Around them lay books on dinosaurs and fossils, posters, and many different types of fossils.

> CLARA: *(authoritatively, displaying a page of a book to the others)* These are the animals we're looking for. I want you all to take a look.
> MAURA: *(speaking with a British accent and pointing to the fossil she is uncovering)* Look, Clara, over here, it's completely flat.
> CLARA: I'm not sure what that is.
> MAURA: This is way too special for people to have. *(She picks up a book and points to a picture.)*
> CLARA: That is not the same as the picture.
> MAURA: Oh my gosh! I think it's a T-Rex! We're going to be famous!

These kinds of observations helped me to more clearly define the kind of work I had seen Emily doing 2 years earlier in her conversations with, and pursuit of, insects. When I recorded the fieldnotes that open this book and this chapter, I did so because I knew Emily was working with her imagination. I was not thinking at the time about the relationship between her imaginative work and the scientific process. Clara and Maura, however, as well as the dramatic play of my other students, helped to direct my attention to the connection between imagination and the development of the scientist's persona.

Here, for example, Clara and Maura were working with identity on two levels. First, they were orchestrating a performance about the work of paleontologists and taking on what they perceived to be the appropriate tone and posture for that work. Then, as part of that process, they were relating to their material—that is, the props in the museum—in a scientific way. Note Clara's statement as she compares the bones being uncovered with the drawing of the dinosaur in the book: "That" (meaning what Maura was uncovering) "is not the same as the picture." Clara used her analytic skills to propose that the skeletal remains of the mold could in no way be the same as the animal illustrated in the book. As 5-year-olds, these girls were beginning to play out a process that Medawar (1982) points to in his description of the actions of scientists:

> Scientific reasoning is therefore at all levels an interaction between two episodes of thought—a dialogue between two voices, the one imaginative and the other critical; a dialogue . . . between the possible and the actual, between proposal and disposal, between what might be true and what is in fact the case. (p. 46)

I now see that like Maura and Clara, Emily also became the scientist in her play with insects and was using many of the tools that scientists might employ as she worked with them, with me, and with her peers. She observed her insects and bugs meticulously, sketched them, recorded details about their development (as we have seen earlier in this book), constructed elaborate environments for them, and spoke authoritatively about their habits. And while an observer might have mistaken her understanding of the role of fantasy when she was talking to her ants and inferred that she was completely immersed in "pretending" (as I most certainly would have prior to this study), Emily was quite clear about what she was doing. When asked if the insects really "talked to her," she admitted that it wasn't really "talk like people do" but that they were "telling" her things. Note the following exchange I had with her one morning before school:

> The principal and I are sitting on a desk chatting as the children begin to come in the room. Emily comes up to us and tells us that her prey-ing mantis has died.
>
> **KAREN:** Did she make an egg case before she died?
> **EMILY:** No, but I asked her if she had laid eggs. And she told me she laid them *before* I caught her.

What I had to conclude, after observing her for a schoolyear, was that the "telling" came from Emily's close and continuous observation of insects.

Emily's work was very congruent with the descriptions we now have from scientists of their childhood experiences of the world. For those who are deeply involved in the study of the natural world, that study often begins at an early age and includes a close and organic relationship with the creatures and the phenomena of that world (Cobb, 1993; Fox-Keller, 1983; Holton, 1973). Yet if we also consider accounts we have of scientists working as adults in the laboratory (Fox-Keller, 1983; Holton, 1973, 1978; Ochs et al., 1996; Rothenberg, 1979; Salk, 1983; Wolpert & Richards, 1997), we find descriptions of imagination working in a different way, one that I believe is also reflected in children's imaginative work. In those accounts, the "I" of self is described as moving into the body of the phenomenon under study. For example, as Sir James Black, a Nobel Laureate, states in discussing his work on beta-blockers:

> You then try and pretend that you are the receptor. You imagine what it would be like if this molecule were coming out of space towards you. What would it look like, what would it do? (quoted in Wolpert & Richards, 1997, p. 126)

Holton (1978) describes how Einstein conceptualized his own thoughts on scientific reasoning to be an intuitive/rational process in which experiences were related to assertions and axioms through a link that was highly intuitive and not easily tracked. Einstein proposed that that link could be seen in his use of an unconscious form "of mental play with

visual materials" (p. 96). An often-cited example of this kind of thinking is Einstein's following account of his work on the special theory of
relativity:

> At that point there came to me the happiest thought of my life, in the fol-
> lowing form: Just as in the case where an electronic field is produced by elec-
> tromagnetic induction, the gravitational field similarly has only a relative
> existence. *Thus, for an observer in free fall from the roof of a house there exists,*
> *during his fall, no gravitational field*—at least not in his immediate vicinity.
> If the observer releases any objects, they will remain, relative to him, in a state
> of rest, or in a state of uniform motion, independent of their particular
> chemical and physical nature. (In this consideration one must naturally neg-
> lect air resistance.) The observer is therefore justified in considering his state
> as one of "rest." . . . The extraordinarily curious, empirical law that all bod-
> ies in the same gravitational field fall with the same acceleration immedi-
> ately took on, through this consideration, a deep physical meaning. (quoted
> in Rothenberg, 1979, p. 113; emphasis in original Einstein quote)

As Emily talked with the insects she captured, lay nose to nose with them
in the dirt, followed them around a play area, and allowed them to crawl
over her body, I believe she was taking on the role of scientist as observer
and taking on the position that Einstein and others describe, that is, working on acquiring the insect's, or object's, point of view. Her work was intuitive and rational, physical and imaginative. Thus, the intersection of imagination with identity has at least two dimensions that are important for our
discussion here: *First, the student takes on the role of the scientist; second, the*
student takes on the point of view of the object or text under study.

As I have learned from Denzel and, later, other children, this process of
identifying with a subject, of being passionate about it, does not occur naturally for all students. I am sure that the reader can name a subject in
school that was difficult or felt undoable—a subject in which the language,
content, and means of expression were almost alien. Traditionally, as students, teachers, and parents we justify those feelings about a subject, and
the subsequent lack of success that often follows, as having to do with "lack
of ability," and we draw a direct line from that observation to intelligence
and aptitude. "Some people," we say, "are just scientific."

However, after studying imagination and watching children who have
had no exposure to a subject become engaged with it through their imaginative action, I no longer believe, for example, that my own inability to

understand mathematics or the workings of the engine of my car has to do with a lack of "aptitude." I think it has much more to do with whether I have made, or can make, personal, imaginative contact with the world of mathematics or the dynamics of engine combustion, whether I can develop a passionate connection with those "texts" and systems and bring them from the outside world into my *internal, schematic system of beliefs and practices.* What would it take, I wonder, for each of us to become engaged with the undoable subject—to identify with it, to become passionate in its pursuit?

CHAPTER 5

"I Am the King Shabazz!":
Appropriating a Discourse
Through Imaginative Action

Tommy: *(listening carefully to the story, maintaining eye contact with the book)* I'm the King Shabazz! [the main character in the book] . . . They always say *man.*

Peter: *(to Tommy)* Do you have glasses like that? [meaning like King Shabazz]

Tommy: *(He nods his head "yes" but does not look away from the book. The story ends.)* I like that story.

Sarah: Why?

Tommy: They keep on saying, "Man." *I* say, "Man. Oh, man!"

Peter: I like that story because it reminds me of when Tommy and me play war.

Tommy: 'Cause they were like us, me and Peter.

Two years after I taught Denzel, on the first day of school when I sat down with my new first graders to read our story, I spotted Tommy. Like Denzel, Tommy mentally checked out as soon as I opened the storybook. My field-notes from early in the schoolyear describe how he looked during story time:

> It is clear from Tommy's story-time behaviors that he just doesn't know how to listen to a story. He looks around, rarely attends to text, watches his friends, plays with his shoelaces. (Fieldnotes, September 8)

I soon found out that Tommy had many things in common with Denzel: He, too, came from a working-class family and had not been read to at home. He, too, was eager, healthy, and respectful but had great difficulty understanding how to focus on the purpose, or the intention, of a lesson in any new area. For example, in math Tommy did not easily master new strategies for computation in addition, such as counting up or using Cuisinaire rods to symbolically represent an algorithm. He found it difficult to use books as resource materials. Also like Denzel, Tommy was very physical, excelling in sports and movement, but he struggled in reading, not having even the most basic kindergarten skills to put to work, although he had attended kindergarten the previous year.

In opening this chapter with an account of Tommy's work in first grade, I hope to look more closely at the idea of literacy and its relation to reading texts of all kinds. I want to show how the process of discourse appropriation is constructed with a series of imaginative building blocks, many of which are laid in place early in a child's education, both at home and at school. I begin with a close look at reading and related language activities. In the latter part of the chapter, I introduce examples that extend my argument into other areas of study.

TOMMY'S WORK WITH TEXTS

Each day when story time arrived, Tommy immediately turned his attention to something else. This time, however, unlike during my early experience with Denzel, I was ready for him. The reader will recall from Chapter 3 how, in September of that new schoolyear, I had changed several aspects of my instructional design and my teaching to reflect what I had learned from Denzel. For example, I offered many more opportunities for retelling of stories using drama, art, and story boards. I allotted more time to basic expressive opportunities—such as building with blocks, painting, clay work, and especially creative dramatics—to help all the children extend their expressive potential and develop their own stories about new topics or about texts that we were studying.

After I saw that Tommy did not listen to stories, I encouraged him to spend a great deal of his time each day participating in these activities, especially in acting out the stories we had read as a class and retelling them on the story board, in the block-building area, and through drawing and painting. I wanted him to connect his way of being in the world with the world of the stories, so that he could feel the stories in his body and then learn to join them with words from books and with his own words.

Drawing

Early in the year, I became concerned about Tommy's work in his art journal. Every morning, before our day officially started, the children drew in their journals for 15 to 20 minutes. Tommy's drawings were almost incoherent in the sense that neither he, Sarah, nor I could decipher what the pictures were about. Figure 5.1 offers an example of Tommy's artwork.

FIGURE 5.1. One of Tommy's drawings

Because Tommy's drawings puzzled and worried me, each morning as he drew I would talk with him as he worked. It became clear to me that drawing was primarily a gross-motor exercise for Tommy. He would often not be able to tell me what the picture was until he began to talk as he drew. Then the picture became a story, but always a story with movement and an almost indecipherable final image. Even though Sarah or I would sit and talk with Tommy either before or while he drew, we saw little change in his art throughout the fall. For example, on December 5, as I watched him draw (see Figure 5.2), I wrote the following notes:

> Tommy has started drawing. He has put a rectangle around the edge of the paper and is drawing house-shaped images in different parts of the rectangle. I ask him what it is. He says, "It's houses."
>
> "What's the square?" I ask.
>
> "To make it safe," he answers.
>
> "Like a border," I say.
>
> "Yeah."
>
> He continues to draw. At each point when he starts a new section, I ask him what it is. XXXX's in a circle are "dead ends"; blues are "earth." Then he starts to do his random scribble (right side/middle) and I say, "Now what's that?"
>
> "I don't know," he answers.
>
> I ask him to stop and think, and say, "If you don't know what it is, don't draw anything." He stops, looks long, then says, "It's a house," makes the scribble into smoke, then adds a roof and windows. He continues drawing. At every point I ask him to explain to me what he's doing. As he finishes, we put notes on the picture showing what each part is.
>
> Then, pointing to the center of the picture, he says, "Those are the bows they tie the ship to. I made the Japanese writing."
>
> When he is done I say, "This is quite a story. Are your other pictures stories, too?" He says "yes" and begins to turn the pages, explaining the stories for each picture. I can tell, however, that the stories are made up and then changed as he physically retraces the lines on the page with his finger. Often as he looks at an old picture, he starts to add lines and scribbles to go with the story he's making up. (Field-notes, December 5)

FIGURE 5.2. Tommy's December 5 drawing

My fieldnotes from that day record my bewilderment over what Tommy was doing in his art as well as a growing sense that the lack of organization in his pictures and his difficulty talking about them might have something to do with his lack of exposure to books and stories:

I think the issue is that he's never spoken his stories. In other words, the images (he's seeing and drawing) have never been told. Does this also come from the same place as not having been read to, not having drawn pictures in your home and having had someone ask, "So, what's happening in that picture?" (Fieldnotes, December 5)

I began to see a little progress just at the point that I thought we were going down a dead end. On December 6, Sarah reported to me that Tommy drew a circle on his page, decided it was the earth, and completed the earth. Sarah left him and when she returned, he had filled in all around the earth, obscuring it as he usually did. However, when I interviewed him later about the picture, he once again identified it as a picture of the earth.

Gradually, Tommy spontaneously told stories about his pictures when Sarah and I talked with him. The pictures themselves were not particularly coherent, but he would "tell" them as he drew. My notes record this process.

Today school started late. When I came into the classroom, he was drawing what clearly was a genie. As he talked, he continued to draw genies, filling in a narrative in connection to the movement of his marker. He drew several genies of different sizes, then said, "This one's younger. This one's a baby," etc. At one point he said as he drew, "This is a bad one," and drew a bad-looking face. Finally he started to draw a person. "This is the kid who opened the bottles." The whole drawing was an evolving story. I participated in extending the story by asking if they gave wishes, what he and Brian (who was drawing next to him) would wish for, saying what I would wish for. Nat added a connection to Aladdin that they liked. (Fieldnotes, December 14)

Story Time

But what was happening in story time? In December my notes record that Tommy still found it difficult to settle and focus during story time. He wanted to please me and listen, but he had trouble sustaining his attention and looking at the pictures unless he was cued to do so by a teacher. Yet he had improved since September and October, and he was doing better than Denzel had done. His attention would move in and out of the story, and he would respond only to some of the pictures. But it did appear that the bridge from his world to the world of school and books and literacy was under construction. So something was happening. Pictures and words were becoming stories. Tommy was planning the story in his head before he drew, and we were beginning to be able to tell what he was drawing before he told us. By January, I noticed that when he shared a picture from his journal with the class, his interactions with the children produced a coherent story. In the sharing chair he was, as Denzel had been, spontaneous, cracking jokes, and confident. He didn't "read" his pictures as a complete whole. Rather, his "reading" came from energy created between himself and his audience. The picture became an opportunity to tell a story for his viewers. The following transcript shows the development of his use of his pictures:

> **Tommy:** This is my night picture, and this stuff makes the dark glow, and this is a cat's head, and this is a pirate's head. That's his patch for his eye. And this is a earth what has eyes. And I'm going to let you guess if it has three eyes.
> **Question:** What are those wavy things around?
> **Tommy:** It's a frame.
> **Question:** What is that *(pointing to a figure)*?
> **Tommy:** That's a guy. He's trying to electrocute himself. (Fieldnotes, January 5)

I continued to watch Tommy in story time. Gradually he listened more to the stories, although he rarely stayed tuned in during an entire reading. I continued to direct him to a variety of expressive activities so that he would process what he'd heard or seen in ways that built the connections from his life to our life in school. As his drawings and storytelling took on more of a narrative form, he showed evidence of identifying on a deeper level with the characters in his picture and with the characters in books. For example, my fieldnotes refer to a drawing from February (Figure 5.3):

> Tommy has been drawing quite a long time. I ask him what he's drawing. He says, "A person." Then I ask why some of the people look so sad. He explains that it's a war picture and a bomb is falling. He points out the bomb. I ask about the building: "That's a base," he says. He points out the guy he's working on. "He's a general, and they shot him and hung him up, and they were beating him with their weapons, and blood is running out." I tried to find out where he'd seen or heard this, but he didn't come up with a source. Then he adds in a "good guys tank" shooting up in the air. (Fieldnotes, February 26)

FIGURE 5.3. "War picture"

Becoming a Reader

By June, Tommy's drawings and stories were more organized, and he was beginning to read and do simple addition and subtraction. But did he listen to stories? Well, not all the time. As I watched him, I saw that he took two steps forward and then one step back. I would be astonished to see him listen and respond to a story, and then the next day see that he checked in and out as the story was being read. But I am not describing my research on imagination and the strategies that resulted to show how successful I am as a teacher. Rather, my goal is to present my growing conviction that something like listening to stories, something that appears to be such a simple prerequisite for becoming a reader, results, in fact, from a complex web of experience that lays out an understanding of *story*: a realization that one can make up stories, that an entire story can be contained in a single picture or a poem.

The web of literacy begins with the simple act of putting children in your lap each day and reading one, two, three, or more books; with asking them, "What did you draw today? What's happening in the picture?" It begins with conversations about the "texts" they create when they play: their constructions, their dramas, their mud pies. Reading, therefore, is more than introducing a child to the letters in the alphabet and the sounds that they make, just as math is more than introducing a child to the names of numerals and how to count. Each web of literacy in each and every subject is constructed through a myriad of encounters with the "body" of that subject, and those encounters occur within an imaginative world that is, in turn, fed and enlarged from those encounters. Being a reader begins, first, with becoming part of the story, then becoming the storyteller who has an audience. Achieving literacy in reading, writing, science, history, math, art, music, or any subject depends on the active work of imagination.

Unlike Denzel, Tommy eventually began to interact in an imaginative way with many of the books we read. The transcript that opens this chapter reveals an instance when Tommy became fully engaged with the story of *The Boy Who Didn't Believe in Spring* (Clifton, 1992). That observation took place in March, after 6 months of work in the classroom in which Tommy had had extensive contact with books, performance, storytelling, retellings, and drawing his own stories. As he listened to the book, Tommy was captivated by the fact that he considered the child in the story to be like himself. In that same time period, Sarah and I recorded several other instances of Tommy being engaged with other books, and we also saw a progression in his understanding of how to develop his own stories.

But it would be inaccurate to claim that by year's end Tommy had made a connection with all the stories that he heard or that his growth in this area was a natural, developmental process that did not require constant interventions on the part of his teachers. In fact, as I looked at my data from that year, I saw that both Sarah and I were constantly monitoring

Tommy's involvement in story time (as well as that of other children), and we were both doing a great deal of explicit instruction about books and about the process of being an engaged reader. Thus, in the next part of this chapter, I want to move beyond the idea that becoming imaginatively engaged as a reader begins and ends with the process of identifying with a story or the characters in it, although that is a large piece of the puzzle. By definition, "discourse appropriation" is not something that one can simply be lured into—although that is, I think, how I first defined it when I encountered Denzel. *Appropriating a discourse requires action on the part of the child and on the part of the teacher: action as performers in a drama whose goal is literacy.*

WHAT IS DISCOURSE APPROPRIATION?

> Tommy comes to me and says he's "going to write a poem." He gets a pencil and paper, sits at a table, writes a bit, then asks me how to spell *the*. I stand him up, take him over to the "doozer" list on the wall, and show him the word *the*. He returns to his paper, writes, then comes over to show me. On the page I see "Look ad the bo". He reads it "Look at the bird" but says, "I don't know how to spell *bird*." We sound out the last letter, and he sits down to finish the word, adding a *d*. He folds the paper up and says, "I'm going to write more poems." He walks over to the class library, takes out a copy of an Eyewitness Book titled *Mammals*, and copies that word. Shows me. I read it. "That's like animals," he says. We discuss what a mammal is. Then I walk away and he takes out a book of poetry we had just read and copies that title. A bit later he asks me for an envelope to put the second paper in for his mother. He walks over to Sarah, shows her the paper, and says, "Look, Sarah, these are words." (Fieldnotes, January 4)

In the fieldnotes above, we see Tommy as he begins to take notice of words, poems, and books. Here, he is at an early stage of identifying himself as a reader and a writer; he is just beginning to understand the relationship among the books we read every day, the words we wrote, the pictures he drew, and the purpose of studying those as a form of communication with significant others, such as his mother, myself, or Sarah.

Although I introduced the achievement of identity in the last chapter, thus separating it as a topic from discourse appropriation, it is clear to me that in the process of becoming literate in a discipline, identity and discourse appropriation are intertwined. As the student begins to take on the role and point of view of a reader, a mathematician, an artist, a writer, a geographer, a musician, an actor, a scientist, or a poet, he or she also comes in contact with the *language, tools, texts, and forms of inquiry* specific to that discipline, what has been called the "tool kit" (Wertsch, 1991) of a discourse. *Productive contact* with the language, symbol system, tools, and texts fuels a deeper identification with the discipline, thus increasing the desire to master it, which in turn fuels the desire to have more contact, and so on.

As Tommy began to pay more attention to the books we read and the words we used on paper, he saw that they might have special meaning for him. When he told me he was going to "write a poem," he was acting on an aesthetic response to a book of poetry we had read; he was aspiring to write his own poems. That desire presented a window through which he began to "see" the words that surrounded him and to use those words for his own purposes.

In my research on Science Talks (Gallas, 1995), I learned that my students began to identify themselves as scientific individuals by taking on the voice and the authority of scientists. I defined the process of appropriation at that time as a language-acquisition process, using Bakhtin's (1981) metaphor of the speaker "populating it [the word] with his own intention, his own accent . . . adapting it to his own semantic and expressive intention" (pp. 293–94). In other words, the process of feeling like a scientist, of identifying oneself as "scientific," was grounded in an ability to talk about it with others and become deeply engaged in the work of building theories and applying data to those theories. My students engaged in that process through collaborative discussions with their peers—energetic, free-ranging discussions that consistently employed imaginative devices such as metaphor and analogy to build scientific theories. They also devised, with my help, questions and experiments from those discussions that enabled them to test their theories and, if necessary, revise them.

However, as I expanded my observations of children's imaginative work in response to Denzel and linked those with my understanding of how children used many different forms of expression to deepen their learning (Gallas, 1994), I saw that the process of appropriating the language of a discourse is one that involves both real-life experiences using the language processes of the discipline *and* expressive action. In this process children take control of their world of experience, in some ways metaphorically "eating it" as Nemerov (1978) proposes, so that the events, texts, and tools they encounter in school become part of their consciousness and are re-expressed through the force of their actions:

> The sight of the eye rests on the object. The sight of the mind is never satisfied with that, but wishes to go through the object, relating, transforming, perhaps even eating it so as to make it a part of mind. (p. 90)

Tools and Texts as Imaginative Objects

In schools, when different subjects are taught, there are tools and texts that are specific to each subject. By "tools," I mean the physical objects that enable us to do the work of learning about a subject. Texts are symbolic (semiotic) vehicles through which students gain information and ideas. Lemke (1990) defines semiotics as "systems of meanings [constructed] by using language, mathematics, diagrams, and techniques" (p. 185). In a woodworking class, for example, students use tools such as hammers, nails, screwdrivers, saws, and so on. The texts (semiotics) they read include plans from which they might build a piece of furniture. In science, students learn to use magnifying glasses, microscopes, dissection tools, calibrated beakers and cylinders, scales and weights, fulcrums, and pulleys. They observe and sketch living organisms, prepare slides, carry out experimental procedures, and read and write lab reports. In social studies or history, students use maps, charts, and timelines. They read texts, primary documents, and literature from particular periods; look at photographs, art, and films; and listen to music. All of these are examples of some of the tools and texts of science, woodworking, and history. Access to them both promotes literacy and fuels imaginative identification with a subject.

Tools and texts, though, are not just inanimate objects. Earlier in the book, we met Emily, who had a unique relationship with ants and other insects. If given the opportunity, all young children, like Emily, become deeply and imaginatively involved with the objects they are using; *they interanimate them, as it were, mingling their imaginative worlds with the object itself.* I take this idea from Bakhtin's (1981) work on language, in which he characterizes the vitality of utterances as occurring at their point of contact with the other: "Discourse lives . . . beyond itself, in a living impulse toward the object" (p. 292). In other words, the tools and texts of a subject gain their vitality when they are brought into *productive* contact with a student's experience.

I emphasize the word *productive* here, as I did earlier in the chapter when referring to Tommy's response to poetry, to point out the need for students in any subject to have real-life experiences with a subject: Textbooks, workbooks, and worksheets, when used as the sole tools and texts of instruction, do not, in my opinion, provide productive contact with a subject. They are, as Bakhtin might put it, "dead." They cannot convey the vitality of reading, writing, science, history, math, or geography.

When students have productive contact with tools and texts, their use of those objects changes over time to mirror what we might expect of literate experts. For example, although Emily did have an imaginative relationship in which she had conversations with insects, she also had a more clinical perspective on her subjects. In the fieldnotes below, we can see that perspective.

> The question is "How do the butterflies change inside the chrysalis?"
> After the talk everyone writes and draws their ideas about the answer, then we discuss how someone might find out the answer to our question. Emily says, "You could take one of them and cut it open and see what's happening inside."
> I say, "That would kill it though, right?"
> Emily says, "Yes, but there are so many of them all over the world that one wouldn't make a difference." She goes on to tell me about a caterpillar she had had whose head got split open. It was quite a clinical description. (Fieldnotes, Science Talk, June 5)

Emily understood that insects of all kinds were texts she could "read" in two different ways. Her imaginative play with them helped her understand their behavior and habits; her clinical attitude toward them made them expendable for the purpose of answering important questions.

Chapter 4 has already described the ways in which practicing scientists interanimate the phenomena they are studying and in that process of deep identification make theoretical discoveries. In my opinion, the process for children is no different. They bring the tool or text to life, as it were, at the same time as they are use them to "practice" and master a subject. And while each subject has a range of different tools/texts that must be mastered, the process of mastery, like the process of using words to make sentences and sentences to make stories, begins first with play and exploration—with the student's appropriation of the tools for his or her own purposes—and moves, as the student's interaction with a subject deepens, toward a more clinical use of the tools. In another example, my fieldnotes show Sasha handling a book as an expert, in the same way that Emily handled her insects:

> As school ends, we have a reading from *A Light in the Attic* (Silverstein, 1981). Sasha comes to me with a page opened to a particular poem she had heard at home and asks me to read it. She walks away briefly and then returns immediately, with the book open to another poem. She says, "I also like this one, and wanted you to read it more than the other one." I asked her how she found the poem so quickly in such a thick book. She answered that she didn't know, she just had. Note here the ease with which she handles books. It's like territory she knows her way around, what might be called a local geography of books. They are familiar to her. This one more so because she's handled it before at her house and she loves the poems it holds. (Fieldnotes, February 29)

From my observations, when students have opportunities to work with real tools and texts, and when those opportunities include exploratory play and independent work, the tools move from being inanimate objects to resources for the development of imagination, identity, and competence. The most easily cited examples I would provide come from early readers and writers. Most of us have observed young children spontaneously using scribbled lines on a page to represent words and sentences before they actually begin to use letters. In this case, the idea of the word as a tool and as a text is used to imaginatively take on the identity and the "work" of the writer, which is to put lines of words on a page. Similarly, children who have been exposed to books since early childhood will pick up a book and "read" the story, even if it is not a known one, as Barbara is doing in the observation that follows:

> Barbara is reading a book about bunnies—very focused. When I ask her what she is reading she says, "Well, I can't read, but I just look at the pictures for a really long time and then make up the words." (Fieldnotes, October 3)

In another example, Donaldo, a first grader whose primary language was Spanish, picked up an unfamiliar nonfiction text on birds to "read" one morning. In fact, when he read this text, he was actually singing it as he turned the pages, basing his song on the pictures in the book:

Cowntry birds
red birds
orange birds
white birds
eat all day.
The bark [tree branch] is so long
it's like a stick
and there's a mouse [squirrel]
Sometime some eat wood.
The bird thinking
but mom took home birds.
They went inside
or outside.
The birds fly!

Thus, for students who would be readers, the book is at first an imaginative object through which they take on the role of a reader. It is an object, to be sure, but it lives. However, as we have learned from Denzel, books do not live for all children, and when that is so, certain essential properties of the reading process fall away and are lost to view.

Action and Discourse Appropriation

Emily walks in from recess carrying her latest project. "I'm almost finished," she says in her professor's voice. "I've got to show Nat."
   "What is it?" I ask.
   "A worm house," she says. The device is a long rectangular tube with open ends. She shows Nat and walks away. (Fieldnotes, October 10)

If given the opportunity to place the world of school into an active, imaginative context, young children begin to appropriate the language, symbols, processes, and tools of the different subject areas for their own purposes. That process of appropriation, though, depends upon the teacher's ability to provide a wide variety of props specific to the subject under study, to provide independent time to use and explore the potential of those props, and to expose students to an array of "cultural tools" (Smagorinsky & Coppock, 1994) that further students' inquiries. Smagorinsky and Coppock include as "cultural tools" writing, drawing, painting, construction, drama, movement, storytelling, and song. I consider these processes of meaning-making to be critical in assisting students as they build the bridge between their experiences of the "now" of classroom texts they come in contact with through the process of instruction and the "future" of new texts that they themselves will create. Emily's construction of a worm house offers an example of how she imaginatively used classroom resources to further her own scientific work.

As students use those processes, they also deepen their use of the language and symbol systems of the subjects they are studying. A universal example from children's play provides an illustration. When I was small, I wanted very much to learn to cook. One Christmas, Santa brought me a baking set, which delighted both me and one of my brothers. We proceeded to bake up a storm. We knew by that time that baking required a recipe, which we made up based on our observations in our home of the real process of baking. We knew that baking required specific measuring tools and ingredients, a timeframe, and a source of energy. We had ready access at first to the boxed mixes that came in my baking set and later (when the boxes ran out) to flour, salt, sugar, and water. Although in no instance did we turn out an edible cake or cookie once the boxed mixes ran out, the process we were engaged in was a basic literacy process and our goal was to become competent as cooks.

In this kind of play can be found the roots of good literacy instruction: previous experience watching a literate other working in the discipline; access to the tools, language systems, and props of the discipline; and opportunities/independent time to explore their uses in an imaginative context.

Observing Literate Others

Story time: Tommy is listening and looking and asking questions to clarify. Appears to check out periodically, losing his focus, but I notice that both he and Peter respond to my cues as I read the story. If I respond to the text and pictures dramatically and "ooh" and "ahhh," he looks up as if awakened from a daydream and comes back in contact with the text. (Fieldnotes, May 14)

Neither Denzel nor Tommy came to school having had experiences at home with books. They had not observed adults reading; they had not been read to by the adults or significant others in their lives. However, it is important to point out that while lack of exposure to books and readers can have serious consequences in many subjects, many children who enter school also have not been exposed to adults doing math or science, adults writing stories and reports, adults playing music or making art, and so on. Thus, the role of the teacher as an explicit model of a literate other is critical. In this sense, if we consider the ways in which we have defined discourse—walking, talking, thinking, acting, studying—mastering a practice involves appropriating a wide range of behaviors and actions within a social context. Teachers, as the experienced literate others, must act as scientist, mathematician, artist, and writer so that their students have opportunities to "apprentice" themselves in those disciplines under the guidance of an experienced practitioner within a supportive community. That is, teachers must themselves strive to understand and be grounded in the literate practices of each subject they teach so that they can model engagement with those practices for their students. As Lave and Wenger (1991) point out:

> Apprentices gradually assemble a general idea of what constitutes the practice of the community . . . who is involved; what they do; what everyday life is like; how masters talk, walk, work, and generally conduct their lives; how people who are not part of the community of practice interact with it; what other learners are doing; and what learners need to learn to become full practitioners. (p. 95)

Teacher as Co-Actor

I began to involve myself in this kind of action during the year I spent observing imagination in first grade. (See Chapter 3.) Part of our math time every week that year included working with estimation and problem solving. The first thing I noticed was that successfully solving math problems required the children to invent a strategy to solve the problem. For example, early in the year I began using our snack foods as material for those activities. On one day in October, I had 32 cookies to distribute among 14 children. The question I asked was: "How many cookies would each child get, and how many would be left over?" We decided to use plastic links to represent each cookie. As I showed the children how each link represented each cookie by laying a link next to a cookie, I noticed that certain children were going blank. I realized at once that I had missed a key point in using the manipulatives. (Recall Denzel's reaction to Cuisinaire rods and other manipulatives in Chapter 1.) There was no connection in the children's minds between the link as a substitute for the cookie.

Similarly, I began to see how the early use of written symbols in math also requires an imaginative leap: The child has to recognize *and believe* that a mark or a check, or even a numeral, can stand for something concrete. For example, in November during a problem-solving activity in which the children were asked to calculate how many ghosts were in a story we had read, Emily was using checks to represent each ghost. She was sitting next to Nat, who was using lines to represent each ghost. Sasha was going down the page listing the numbers, adding in the next number of ghosts, crossing out the previous number, and writing the new total. For example, she would write 10, add 9 in, cross out the 10 and write 19, add in the next number, which was 7, write 26 and cross out the 19, and so on. Each of these examples required a realization on the children's part that the number in the story could be represented symbolically in another way. That understanding depended on imagination to generate a new strategy for problem solving, essentially, as Warnock (1976) points out, enabling us to "treat the objects of perception as symbolizing or suggesting things other than themselves" (p. 10).

The process of performing math stories, however, proved to be more difficult than the process of performing literary stories, even when the math stories emerged from the day-to-day events of our classroom. The children's difficulties with taking on the roles in the problems persisted whether the problem was one I took from a math book or one we posed from a classroom event. One day in March, after having little success with the performances of story problems, I realized that I had to intervene by taking on one of the roles in the math dramas.

> The problem reads: "Four fish line up to use the diving board. The red fish is first in line. The blue fish is in front of the yellow fish. The green fish is in front of the blue fish. What color is the last fish in the line?" Peter is reading the problem. I figured this would be an easy problem to act out. The boys (Chinua, Brian, and Tommy) stay seated on the ground and don't react to the reading. Peter reads the problem again. No one moves or talks. I tell them I want them to act it out to solve it. They attempt to act it out but without using any words. So I directly intervene and take on the role of one of the colored fish in the story, talking my way through the part. This actually works; they

become the other fish and quickly solve the problem. I realize that acting it out with myself as a character helped to animate the problem. (Fieldnotes, March 12)

That movement on my part from coach to co-actor had an immediate impact on all their performances in math. As they saw Sarah and me participating as collaborators with them, the children were more able to develop coherent stories and actively take on a role in the stories. At this point I began to understand the need for me to take on more than a coaching or bystander's role and to become a co-actor. To do that, I had to have an understanding of the action of imagination in the process of solving the problem, and I had to model the role of the literate other working through that process.

OBSERVING THE PROCESS OF DISCOURSE APPROPRIATION

In late September of 1998 I observed the beginnings of an interesting phenomenon in my kindergarten classroom. One morning, a small group of girls noticed a large box of maps that had been placed prominently on a bookshelf since early September, and they decided to go on a "trip." They set up a row of chairs as if they were airplane seats, unfolded the maps, and spent about 30 minutes "going to California." Two weeks later the maps came out again, but this time about 14 children joined in the travel fantasy in groups, segregated by gender. As with the first time, the girls lined up chairs and spent a great deal of time scrutinizing the maps, while the boys sat at tables doing the same. This time, though, they also began to make their own maps, drawing on their laps while they "traveled," as if recording their itineraries. My fieldnotes record their account of what they were doing:

The girls noted that they were on their way to one particular map's "place." It was a map of the Amazon. I opened the map and showed them the whole map. They said they were already on the airplane and were drawing where they would go. I asked Clara what the marks were on her paper, and she said they showed where they would stop. I pointed out on the map of the Amazon how towns were marked.

> The boys said they were going all over the world, and the maps they were using showed the places they would stop. (Fieldnotes, October 19)

I talked to all of them extensively about what they were doing, and they described what part of the journey they were on as well the status of the other trips going on in the other groups.

This second round of map work continued for about 5 days. The children produced piles of maps on their own, sharing them at the end of each morning. As I continued to talk to them about their work, I saw the intense interaction between their work with the maps and their imaginations. They were becoming travelers who used maps to go on hypothetical journeys.

> Sabrina is showing me a map of her flight to Africa. She says she's on the plane and then suddenly she's getting off and, "Whoosh, I'm in the water, swimming!" Clara, Leila, and Maura are still on the "plane," discussing what their names are and the details of their trip.

> **MAURA:** *(to Leila)* You're Rosie, right?
> **LEILA:** There's going to be 19 animals there.
> **CLARA:** And the black mark [on the map] shows where there's all the animals.
> **SABRINA:** *(pointing to her map)* This is the castle, and I'm swimming in the water. The castle was not far away. I got on the plane, drived there *(pointing to the lines on the map she's drawn)*, and then went to the castle. It was not far away.
> *(The other girls continued talking about their itinerary.)*
> **MAURA:** When we get there, we're going to go shopping; we're going to have lunch and have a lot of fun.
> **LEILA:** What's the weather like in Africa?
> **CLARA:** It's hot . . . and very very hot.
> **MAURA:** The next day after we get there it will be snowing.
> *(Charles has joined the map work because I said he couldn't go in blocks today. He comes over to us after drawing a map and tells us he's going to Africa, too.)*
> **KAREN:** What will you do there?
> **CHARLES:** I'm going to go on that jet over there and catch wild rhinos. (Fieldnotes, October 21)

Maps and Discourse Appropriation

In thinking about this episode of map work and its relation to the idea of discourse appropriation, we can see the presence of the factors I discussed earlier in the chapter: contact with the language, tools, texts, and forms of inquiry of a discipline; opportunities for expressive action using those; and access to literate others. In this process, my moves as a teacher had two aspects. The first was that I regularly used maps and globes with the children in large and small groups when we read literature from or about different parts of the country and the world, when someone had gone on a trip, or when we were talking about where, for example, the Loch Ness monster was reported to live. In this process, I acted as the literate other who both showed the children how maps and globes were used and invited them to join me in the talk and inquiry that those tools provoked.

My second move was the way in which I provisioned the classroom space with many different kinds of maps and globes for the children to handle, and, when they began to make their own maps, I (metaphorically) pointed to their growing identities as geographers by talking with them about their motives and intentions as they worked and prompting them to share their new maps at the end of each day. At no time, though, did I ask the children to fill out a worksheet on maps or assign tasks related to criteria I believed they should be mastering. Instead, as they worked with their imaginative scenarios using the maps, I saw them developing a familiarity with the map as a text and a tool, an ease in handling maps and drawing their own, and an ability to look at real maps and globes and discuss the geographic features they represented.

Reimagining the Map as a Text and a Tool

Throughout the year the children returned to the maps intermittently, always using them with three components: imaginary trips, the handling and "reading" of real maps, and the invention of new maps of their own. In March, during their last round of map work, two girls invented a new kind of three-dimensional map, which they made copies of for me when they saw my evident interest in trying to understand what they were doing. Here is how they described their maps and their intentions in designing them:

First we found the maps, and then we wanted to make our own maps. So we copied from the maps how to draw. Then we started to go on a trip, and then we made calculators on our maps! The calculators reminded us of the telephone and then we put on a TV. If we don't have a telephone, we couldn't call, and we needed to count stuff on the calculator. If we say something on it [keypad], like, "Is someone having a birthday party here?" . . . It will say "no" or "yes" and where it [the party] is. We also made a key for the whole world to unlock wherever you go, and to lock it back up whenever you go away. (Fieldnotes, March 18)

The girls also added in a real writing pad for notes. Each of these components, including the keypad, calculator, telephone, and TV screen, was drawn or built onto the maps.

The girls' extension of mapmaking involved a blending of in-school and out-of-school worlds, the former rich in props, texts, and creative arts opportunities, the latter rich in technology, travel, talking toys, and birthday parties. In looking closely at the ways in which their maps evolved, I could see that these 5-year-olds were beginning to take control of the map as both an imaginative text and a tool, reconfiguring both the design and the future of maps in their lives. However primitive the prototypes they were creating, they envisioned maps as three-dimensional, interactive tools existing in cyberspace with physical, personal, and social functions. This work was about imagination and it was also about power, control, and "worldmaking" (Cobb, 1993), all basic elements in the process of becoming literate.

CHAPTER 6

Authoring

Worldmaking is learning in the widest sense, but it is also an adaptation to environment as nature, a search for higher levels of synthesis of self and world drawn from the recognition that outer and inner worlds are interdependent aspects of reality, rather than independent states. (Cobb, 1993, p. 66)

KAREN: Sophia, how do you think of all these stories?
SOPHIA: Oh, I do it all the time.
KAREN: But how do you learn to do it?
SOPHIA: Well, when I go to bed at night, I just begin to make them up, and then it just puts me to sleep and they become a dream.

As the last two chapters have proposed, I believe that the process of discourse acquisition, of identifying with and then taking on the "tool kit" of a subject (Gee, 1996), is on many levels simultaneously a private and public process. In the conversation above between Sophia and myself, it was clear that this 6-year-old prepared and rehearsed her stories when she was at home, but, as this chapter will illustrate, Sophia's stories, when told to the class, took on the flavor of a performance that was directly related to her knowledge of her audience.

When students' interactions with texts, props, and cultural tools are carried out with the awareness that they will have an audience, their actions move into the realm of what I am calling "authoring." The map work I described in the last chapter would not have continued over a 6-month period without the rich social interactions that surrounded it and propelled it forward. The children shared their work at the end of each day. That, in turn, fueled new and different kinds of work both with maps and in other parts of the classroom. The public display and interaction around work products shifted the focus for evaluation, or "valuing" (Richardson,

1964), of the work from myself as teacher to all of us as members of the classroom community.

This kind of sharing of work products in classroom settings is not new, as I pointed out in discussing Richardson's (1964) work in Chapter 3. In the field of language arts, authors such as Paley (1990) and Dyson (1993, 1999) have vividly described the kinds of texts that emerge from the interaction of young writers and storytellers with an audience. In writing workshop the public sharing of texts by student authors with peers is considered to be essential to the development of young writers. However, I seek here to expand the definition of *author* in this process, to illustrate the active point at which the literacy learner, regardless of the subject, makes contact with an audience and is, in turn, propelled forward in his or her understanding of a discipline by that audience. Those interactions are shaped by the social networks of the classroom and by the imaginative worlds of the students as they make contact around texts.

AUTHOR VERSUS AUTHORING

For the purposes of speaking about literacy learning, I believe *the act of being "an author" must be distinguished from the process of authoring.* Bakhtin presents the idea of author as "a creating, not a created, thing; he represents, but is not himself represented . . . he exists primarily in the realm of 'I-for-myself,' which means that he is not part of the world" (Morson & Emerson, 1990, p. 430). In this sense being an author does not necessarily include direct, personal contact with an audience. Yet Bakhtin also identifies a tension in his definition of the author, because although the author's work is created apart from the world, it is also created with an awareness of a future audience, and eventually it comes in contact with a listener or a reader: "The author senses himself not as a person executing a preformed plan but as a person at work over an incomplete task in an open world" (Morson & Emerson, p. 430).

In the work my kindergarten students were doing, though, this dichotomy was not present. Texts were created in constant contact and collaboration with an audience, and that interaction was essential to the development of identity and sustained movement toward discourse appropriation, or mastery of the subject. Thus, I put forth here the term *authoring* to signify the ongoing, public nature of that activity. I am defining authoring as the process of *metaphorically "writing" the world in a way that gives that interpretation of the world weight, voice, and agency—a way that has the ability to influence the thinking, feelings, and actions of others.*

Authoring represents a physical incarnation of imagination as it comes in contact with the world. It is distinguished from more internal, imaginative processes (e.g., reverie, fantasy) because it is a public event in which an individual purposefully presents an original text to an audience. The text can be oral or written, a painting, a dance, or a song; it can be an explanation of the solution to an equation or the presentation of a theory in a discussion about the physical world. The author presents the text to an audience in a public way, essentially for some kind of validation.

Bruner (1986), in discussing the process of being introduced to a culture through education, says that "education, if it is to prepare the young for life as lived, should also partake of the spirit of the forum, of negotiation, of the recreation of meaning" (p. 123). Thus, the path to literacy is not a private, introverted path. It requires interaction with, and validation by, a community of peers. To me, therefore, authoring represents an imaginative leap toward the core of discourse acquisition: one must believe and know, *and* one must convince others. In other words, literacy is a process of merging who we believe we are with what we show we can do.

SHARING TIME AND AUTHORING

Ellie is sharing a design from her art journal.

SOPHIA: What are they supposed to be?
ELLIE: Just designs.
SOPHIA: They look like cherries.
ELLIE: They're designs.
SOPHIA: Could they be flowers?
NAT: They look like spider webs.
SOPHIA: Like in *Charlotte's Web.* I'd be the spider.
JAMILLA: I'll be Charlotte.

As the reader will recall from Chapter 3, when I first began researching imagination in my classroom, I was fortunate to have a class of wildly creative first graders. Often their sharing-time exchanges, like the one cited above, almost organically became opportunities for everyone to brainstorm, free associate, and compose. Within that class, Sophia became a focal child for me as I tried to document how children used the imaginative process in different areas of the curriculum. Sophia was a most remarkable child who seamlessly integrated her imaginative life with the realities of the world around her. Her work in every expressive domain was tremendously compelling; she had a great ability to create complex stories while also holding an audience's attention through the telling of those stories. In her stories, Sophia used many devices: surprise, tonal changes, literary speech, risk, danger, allegory, facial emphasis, and gesture. She used tone, especially, forcefully and skillfully.

The class was quite taken with her stories, and, through her own work, Sophia set a high standard for the storytelling genre. Her classmates had a natural inclination to use objects for sharing, as many young children do, but Sophia continued to come forth with extravagant stories in which an object, if she used one, was the springboard from which the story grew. In that way her friends, who saw how compelling her stories were, were challenged to continue to work on their own pretend stories. In addition, during the "questions or comments" period that followed her stories, Sophia remained completely engaged with her audience. She would look intently into her questioner's eyes, a half-smile on her face, her body either leaning toward the questioner or inclined to the side if he or she was on either side of her. Thus, Sophia presented both artful stories and a model of how to take the "authoring stance" by being actively engaged with, curious about, and responsive to an audience's interpretations of a text.

Sophia as a Storyteller

What follows is one example of Sophia's work. This story offers an example of how she used an improvised story as a vehicle for performance and social control.

> *(Sophia is looking through her art journal to find a particular picture.)*
> **Sophia:** Well, the true story is . . . me and Barbara and my sister and my daddy and mommy had a picnic at Walden Pond. And me and Barbara went into the water. And I go, "1, 2, 3," and went under the water, but did not open my mouth 'cause it's bad-tasting. I'll bring in the sand from there on my next sharing day. The end.
>
> Now I'll tell my fake story. *(She opens to the page and shows the picture.)*

OK. Everybody ready? This is me and Barbara. That's me. This is
Violet [the class bunny], and that's Barbara. Once upon a time, two
little girls . . . *(Some chatter and exclamation begin among the boys.
Sophia pauses dramatically, stares the boys down.)*
Quiet! *My* story.
(She pauses and sweeps the crowd with a challenging look.)
Two little girls . . . and they went into the woods and found a
poor little girl named Julie, and gave her pretty clothes. And they
had a chef named Dum-Dum and they made him a funny hat. And
they had another friend who wore a sombrero. And one day a
handsome young prince came named Tommy. He was gonna pick
the loveliest lady ever *(singsong)*, and that would become his bride
*(crosses her hands over her heart, sighs as if love-struck, and stares
into the distance)*. So he picked the one with the highest heels and
the dress with violets and carrots *(pointing to the picture of herself in
the journal)*. Then another king came, and his name was Allen, and
he married the other girl.
One day Barbara and Sophia wanted to visit. But the two Kingies
did not like that. So they had a battle. But the Queen Sophia took
her King, and she dragged him away to her castle! And wouldn't
let him out, and gave him nothing but oatmeal and water! And
she threw him down a waterfall, where he met King Tommy and
tigers, and ran away.
(pauses, looks around her audience) Actually . . . no. He went
back in his cage and said, "Questions or comments?"
[Later, in response to a series of questions asking her what was
going to happen next, Sophia says:] Then I left and went to get a
dodo bird so I could *squeeze his guts out!*
PETER: Geez, she's really something! (Sharing Time, June 6)

Like all her stories, this story was socially inclusive, using children in the
class as main characters, but Sophia remained clearly in charge of the story
and her performance. Note for example, how she actually got in two stories,
one true and one "fake," giving a preview of what she would do in the following week in sharing time and still getting to tell another story. Note also
her response to the children's distracting chatter early in the text and her
twist on the marriage theme, with the queen having power over the king.
Here, Sophia took a picture from her journal and made up a love story that
started out in a predictable pattern but broke the pattern in the middle to

appeal to the girls in the class and incite the boys. The story also included violence, something Sophia, who was a diminutive, feminine girl, specialized in, a fact that constantly delighted and horrified the boys in the class.

At the time I began watching Sophia I was completing a study of power and gender in the classroom and had been working with the notion of performance and persona as a way to understand the dynamic social life of children in school (Gallas, 1998). I had closely observed Sophia and two other powerful and imaginative girls, Barbara and Jamilla, who also used improvised storytelling to gain influence in the class. These girls solidified my belief that performance was an integral part of children's social interactions, but they also caused me to think more deeply about the concept of audience. I had learned that most children in my first- and second-grade classes were acutely aware of the reactions of their audiences to their social maneuvering. Some even knew, at 6 and 7 years of age, how to control or manipulate their audience. Yet as first graders, Sophia and her two classmates had an understanding of audience that was more fluid. They intimidated, cajoled, charmed, and repudiated their audiences depending on their aesthetic and social purposes. Their understanding of the relationship between audience and performer stood out for me, but at that time I did not draw the connection between those understandings and my inquiry into the imaginative process.

The Listener's Role

> Performance involves on the part of the performer an assumption of accountability to an audience.... From the point of view of the audience, the act of expression on the part of the performer is thus marked as subject to evaluation for the way it is done, for the relative skill and effectiveness of the performer's display of competence. (Bauman, 1977, p. 11)

Every painting, sculpture, performance, poem, story, theory that is presented to an audience begins with an imaginative response to the world, but the desire to communicate that response also involves its own kind of imaginative belief that one can make contact with an audience. Essentially, a student, even one who sits in a chair to share a story or an object with a class, does so at some personal risk. Yet the possibility of risk is somehow overshadowed by the desire to be seen and heard, to be simultaneously provocative and challenged. As any performer, public speaker, researcher, or teacher knows, that kind of risk taking requires a vision, or an imaginative projection, of the role to be played and a giant leap of faith about the merits of the would-be performance and the intentions of the audience. It also is preceded by private rehearsal and visualization of the performance before it occurs. Audiences are not always kind, and audiences of children can be especially brutal toward their peers.

Over the years, as I have watched successive classes create stories for sharing time, I have seen that the storytelling child does one kind of imaginative, synthesizing work that takes skill and thought. The listening children, however, do another kind of imaginative, synthesizing work in order to become part of the story. That work is personal, social, and intellectual. In some cases, their longing to be inside the story is palpable. In my mind, then, creating, writing, or telling a story is, in some ways, an easier endeavor than viewing it from outside. To create means to be in control of the body and the flow of a text. It is in your mind's eye, and you are creating the actions and reality of the story in an omniscient way: Emotions, life history, truths, and distortions flow directly into the story. True, the story develops based on contact with an audience, but the author controls and manipulates the story to reflect her needs and goals.

Audiences, therefore, in trying to understand a text, must strive to make someone else's reality their own. They must wrap themselves into the story and make sense of the author/performer's motives, feelings, perspectives, and understanding of the world. Audience members try to gain some control over a story by drawing upon their own life experience and understanding of reality; they search for a hook to hang their hat on. Unfortunately, however, as we have seen with Denzel and Tommy, especially when they encountered stories in books where the teller was absent, sometimes there is no hook and the story never comes to life.

A NEW SETTING

In 1998, I moved to California and took a job teaching kindergarten in a small rural charter school on the central California coast. My interest in exploring the manifestations of imagination continued in this new setting, and I was able to expand my data collection to include 5-year-olds. The 20 children in my class were predominantly European American, with one African American child and one child who was half Inuit and half European American. Socioeconomically, the children were primarily from middle- and upper-middle-class homes, with a large percentage of mothers who were not working outside the home and only three families with divorced parents. Of my 20 students, all but 4 had attended preschool for at least 2 years. The 4 children who did not attend preschool—Sabrina, George, Joe, and Margie—were from families with limited incomes. I identify these children because, as the reader will see, their work in kindergarten, especially when considered in the context of this chapter and my evolving questions about imagination and literacy, provided a significant contrast to that of their peers.

In September of 1998 I began to tape sharing time, as I have done since 1989. I sat and waited for the children's stories to emerge in my kindergarten and offered many different kinds of opportunities for storytelling and dramatic performances. Nothing happened. My students were active in drama and blocks—they were making up stories in the contexts of their play in those areas—but when faced with an audience of their peers, they did not naturally tell a story about anything. In fact, they had little to say at all. There were, however, a few notable exceptions: Sabrina, Margie, George, and Joe.

In the second week of school, Sabrina, Margie, and George began to use the last period of our morning—the part I called "story and songs"—for performances. These began one day in response to my query as to whether anyone had a song to sing for the class. I had said it could be a song they had already learned or one they just made up. In response, Sabrina immediately stood up and asked if she could sing "a song about love." She began to sing and directed me to play my guitar as she sang. As I changed chords, she naturally changed her song lines to accompany me, completely improvising lyrics and melody. The other children were quite surprised and clapped when she was done. I then asked for another song, and Margie got up and sang a song about the sky and the clouds. When she was done, the children clapped and I asked Margie if she had made up the song or been taught it, and she said she had made it up. At that point, George, who had pointedly said he did not like songs and had climbed up in the loft while the girls were singing, came down and signaled that he, too, had a song. He came over to me and directed me to play, and as I started he began to do a beautiful martial arts dance. The children were completely taken aback and thought he was being funny, and some began to laugh. George stopped dancing and began to cry. When I explained to George that the children were just surprised by his dance, he dried his tears and said he'd try again. He had not drawn a distinction between the words *song* and *dance,* and had interpreted the girls' songs and his own desire to move to my guitar chords as congruent. He then performed another dance, which the other children were able to watch and appreciate.

This event began to recur regularly with the same three children and, on some occasions, Dan, as regular performers. The rest of the class continued to watch, but they were unable to create these kinds of spontaneous texts. In mid-November I recorded the following:

> Sabrina sings, "Five mice built a home for their mother in the snow." Melodic and quiet with clear words. George sings a song about three wolves and how they built a house in the woods of different things. Pigs are mixed in, as is the element of the three houses in "The Three Little Pigs." Dan also sings a song today that actually is a summary of the book we just read, *Frederick,* by Leo Leonni. His song is actually about Frederick and the field mice living in the snow. Still, those three plus Margie are the only ones that make up songs.

In light of my experience with children like Sophia and other classes of young children in Brookline who moved easily into storytelling and performance, this class's silence and passivity surprised and puzzled me. However, there were a few differences between this class of kindergartners and the children I had taught in Brookline that may have provided the contrast. These children were a year younger, and most had gone to traditional preschools that offered a curriculum focused on basic reading and math skills. In contrast, the children I taught in Brookline had experienced progressive, developmental kindergartens that focused on language development, socialization, and play.

Beginning the Authoring Cycle

Still, the efforts of Sabrina, Margie, and George now represent to me a first movement into the authoring cycle, one I was probably more able to see because of the accompanying silence of their peers. The class's work in sharing time, though, did not change in spite of my modeling both the sharer's role and the audience members' role: None of the children were able to create expanded oral texts of any kind. Rather, they took a passive stance, presenting an object to the class with a few short sentences—for example, "This is my rock; I got it at the beach"—and then waiting for the class to respond. The children were active in drama, blocks, painting, and unstructured dramatic play, but virtually all of their work in these areas was private work. Each time I attempted to pull the private dramas into the public space by offering opportunities for spontaneous plays or for sharing their performances, they could not make the transition.

A few slight changes occurred in late October, initiated again by Sabrina and Margie, with the addition of Joe. These three children began to co-construct shared texts using the sharing child's toy or picture as a vehicle. Sabrina, Margie, and Joe spontaneously created stories as part of their response to the sharer's text. Here are three sharing-time texts that illustrate how this kind of response developed over a 3-week period:

TROY: *(He shares a picture of a spaceship from his art journal. He asks for questions or comments.)*
SABRINA: *(stands up and turns to face the group)* He and his dad went out in space, and another ship came to find him.
JOE: Some aliens in my spaceship came, and we couldn't get down. We threw knives on the window. One dropped out of the window and we threw knives at it. (Sharing Time, October 30)

This brief exchange marked the first time that any child had attempted to form a story in the public space of sharing time. In this case, Sabrina and Joe used the sharing child's picture as a springboard for truncated stories. Sabrina's physical act of standing up as if to address the group also underscored her sense that this was a performance in which she was formally claiming a role. In this instance she literally took the stage by standing next to Troy as she spoke.

MARGIE: *(sharing a picture from her art journal)* This is my mom and me. I'm out in the field in my dress with my mom. Questions or comments.
LEILA: Karen, could you read what you wrote [on the picture]?
KAREN: *(reading the written text below the picture)* I am going to get my bathing suit on.
ROBERT: Did you go boogie boarding?
MARGIE: Yes, and I got knocked off my board, and a wave as big as this school came and cracked me. And I could stand on my boogie board. And I did something you can't do that I did.
CHILDREN: What's that?
MARGIE: I can do a back flip on my boogie board.

CHILD: My brother can do that.

JOE: Once on my boogie board, I saw this big wave coming, so I let
go of the rope and balanced until I got on the wave. And the
wave was bigger than this building. And the wave sailed all the way
to [??]. I surfed and it was as big as this whole class standing on top
of the whole class, standing on top of each other. (Sharing Time,
November 4)

In this case, Margie presented an initial explanation of her text and then,
in responding to my reading of her dictation, developed a more expanded
storyline based on her original intention in drawing the picture. In
response to her comment, Joe then improvised a story that paralleled
Margie's. It was both responsive to the intention of her text and broader
in its use of hyperbole.

And finally, the following text marked the beginning of a kind of interactive storytelling style that began to occur in different forms through the
agency of these four children with the addition of Dan.

GEORGE: *(sharing a toy bat)* This is my bat, and this it's tail. I got this
at Burger King. Questions or comments.

DAN: Which Burger King? The one that has a lot of hamburgers?

GEORGE: The one with chicken.

SABRINA: What movie is he [the bat] from?

GEORGE: *Anastasia.*

DAN: Once there was a bat and he lived in the rain forest.

MARGIE: And a dinosaur came and almost ate him and he flew so fast
he couldn't ate him.

SABRINA: One time there was Anastasia in the movie and the guy had
a hat like that.

JOE: There was some long teeth sticking out of the tree, and it was a
T-Rex.

[George had been trying to speak but the speakers were coming in
too fast for him to intervene.]

KAREN: George, would you like to try one?

GEORGE: Yes. There was a dog named Ruby (the name of my basset
hound), and a dog named Ruby found a bat. This bat. This one I
have in my hand. *(George smiles broadly, and the children laugh
out loud.)* (Sharing Time, November 11)

Developing an Awareness of Audience

During this same time period, Joe, who is a gifted artist, began to use the sharing chair as a vehicle to feature his art and tell long stories that held the children in thrall. Following is an example of the kind of text he would create:

> **JOE:** *(sharing a book he has illustrated at home, quite long, about 20 pages of drawings)* This is a Utahraptor book. The kind like in Jurassic Park. This raptor isn't real. He's a robot.
> *(Children begin to comment and talk about the first picture.)*
> **MARK:** Can everybody hold their comments!
> **JOE:** *(pointing to page 1)* Does he look happy? He ate a dinosaur.
> *(page 2)* He's dunking down, so nobody can see him. When people come by, he's jumping out.
> *(page 3)* You think that's how big a T-Rex is to a person? [See Figure 6.1.]
> *(page 4)* Lookit what I got in there. Lookit what the man threw in there! Threw a bomb. Do you think it's going to blow up a robot?
> *(page 5)* Lookit! The toy robot. That's the thing his toy robot does. Lookit what's coming up ahead! A raptor shadow!

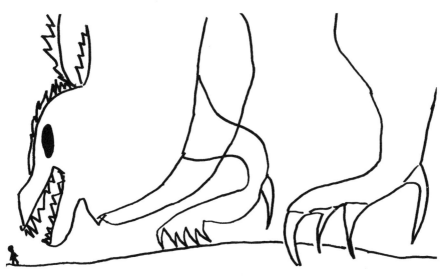

FIGURE 6.1. "You think that's how big a T-Rex is to a person?"

(The class's comments are getting quite rowdy, with action noises going on and lots of talk about the art.)
JOE: I'm not going on until everyone is quiet.
(The group immediately quiets down.)
JOE: *(page 6)* Do you think that thing is gonna kill . . .
(suddenly looks up at his audience, wide-eyed, making a funny face)
    Whoops! I forgot to draw his head! (Sharing Time, November 19)

Joe's performances began to resemble the work I had seen Sophia and her friends doing 2 years earlier in my first-grade class in Brookline. Although Joe lacked Sophia's fluency and skill as a storyteller, his intentions in influencing and controlling the audience through his art were well defined. In this case, he used the turning of the pages to control the pace of his narrative and the amount of time he had as the presenter, much as Sophia had used props to create tempo in her performances. Later, he stopped the momentum he had created to restore order so that the audience could once again focus on his drawings: "I'm not going on until everyone is quiet." As an artist, he had learned through previous sharing experiences that his illustrations anchored his audience's attention and gave him status in the class.

Going Public

In spite of the storytelling performances of these few children, the rest of the class did not begin to make a similar shift toward creating public stories. However, a few changes occurred in the first week of December. Three girls—Clara, Bobbie, and Leila—found a box of blank cards, envelopes, shipping labels, and stationery in the writing center and began to use them, writing letters to each other and to their moms, stuffing the shipping labels (which they called "checks") in the envelopes, and sealing them. That same day, Leila and Bobbie were in the house with Sabrina, lying on the floor dressed in bouffant skirts, hats, and high heels, staring at themselves in the mirror. I overheard them talking about their hotel and restaurant, and I casually walked over to ask them if they needed a business manager to help them. After asking me what a business manager was, they were unanimously in favor of the idea, and I sat down with them and took their dictation, writing up a menu with prices. They then took an order from me, and I was served tea and muffins.

The next day at our reading meeting I showed the menu and asked the girls to describe their restaurant. I also asked the letter writers to describe their activities. At choice time that day, there were more developments. Robert and Troy, who had never before shown an interest in the drama corner, went right to it, set the table for the restaurant, got me to tie carpenter aprons around their waists, went to the writing center and picked up some "checks," wrote their names on the checks, and pasted them to the front of their shirts. Several other children went to the writing center and began to compose "letters," mostly pictures for their mothers, using copious amounts of envelopes and stickers for stamps.

Again I visited the restaurant and asked for a table. The boys were quite surprised and asked me why I was there. I said I was there to eat and was waiting for a friend to join me. Robert escorted me to a table, gave me the menu, and waited for my order. I noted that he didn't have a pad to take my order on and went and got him a thick, short pad of paper. As I ordered from the menu, he carefully copied down the words and prices, then tore the paper off the pad and passed it to Troy, who cooked the meal. By that time they were joined by Dan, who served me my meal. Before I ate, I asked for a telephone, saying I needed to make a call. Once again they were quite surprised, but they handed me the phone. Here is my text:

> Hello. Yes, this is Karen. Well, where are you? I've been waiting a long time, and I'm hungry. I don't care if you're stuck in traffic; we had a date and you're very late. Well, I'm just going to go ahead and order. Bye.

The boys had listened to the whole conversation, as had Sabrina, who had joined me at the table—dressed in a hat, purse, gold-sequined shoes, and purple cape—and was waiting to be served. Dan served my "shrimp" and then went over to the phone, picked it up, dialed a number, and proceeded to have the following conversation

> **DAN:** Are you bringing that stuff we need? When will it get here? OK. Tell me when you're here and I'll come and unload the truck.

A short time later, Sabrina asked for the phone, dialed, and began a conversation as her meal was served.

At the time I was only slightly conscious of the relation between my decision to join in the drama with the children and my desire for them to bring their private dramas into the public domain. Later, in looking at the outcome of these series of events and in further defining what authoring meant to me, I realized that the teacher and the teacher-researcher were acting in concert as the "literate other" (see Chapter 5). I had become a co-actor in order to pull their performances into the public, or official, world of the classroom. My performances enabled many children to expand their own, and, further, my request that the products or texts of their dramatic work be shared had a snowball effect. In essence, these 5-year-olds began to widen their lens and take notice of what was around them; they began to see what Joe, Margie, George, and Sabrina already knew—that there were personal and public benefits to working with an audience. (Or perhaps I might propose that the other children began to remember what they had once known but had forgotten, or unlearned, in preschool.)

Co-Constructing Performances

The following week, sharing time began to change. What changed, however, was not that the sharing children began to tell stories, as I had expected, but rather that performances were co-constructed between the sharing child and the audience, using the object or picture that the sharing child was presenting. In most cases, what was developing was a comedic series of exchanges in which the sharing child played the fool while also explaining the picture being shared or adding detail to the description of an object. The exchanges began to resemble the ways in which Sophia had used pictures, props, and the social dynamics of her audience to orchestrate a performance. This time, though, every member of the audience participated in responding to the text and shaping the performance of the sharing child. The following example was orchestrated by Margie with the help of her audience.

> **Margie:** *(sharing her art journal)* This is me. This is my dog with a tree. These are the flowers and the little birdies. Questions or comments.
> **Sabrina:** Where's the sun?
> *(Margie looks and points to the corner of the picture.)*
> **George:** Well, I used to have a dog, but it old.
> **Thomas:** Um, why is your head so tall?
> *(Margie turns the book around, stares carefully at the picture, looks up and laughs as she shrugs.)*

Leila: Um. Um. Where's your body? I see just your hair, but . . .
(Margie points to the body, which is yellow and hard to see from the audience.)
Justin: It looks like you're gone, 'cause the sun, it's so bright!
Joe: You're disappearing!
Margie: *(turns the book around, stares at it for several seconds, looks up as if surprised)* Ahhh!
(The class laughs out loud.)
Sabrina: It looks like you're all yellow!
Margie: *(turns the book around, stares, looks up with the same look of surprise)* Ahhh!
(Once again the class laughs, this time louder.)
Brian: I can't see your eyes and your mouth.
Margie: That's because they're too light.
Sabrina: Are you throwing a ball for your dog?
Margie: Yeah.
Sabrina: I don't see the ball!
Margie: *(looks briefly at the book, then up at her audience)* Ahhh!
(The crowd laughs again.)
Joe: Where's your nose?
Margie: *(same routine)* Ahhh!
Dan: That's a good tree. But why didn't you draw the branches?
Margie: *(turns the book, stares harder, looks up, eyes wider)* Ahhh!
(The class breaks up. Boys are rolling on top of each other. Girls are hugging each other with excitement.) (Sharing Time, December 10)

In the days that followed, Margie's "Ahhh!" routine was adopted and adapted by a few other children for their own purposes. The children introduced extensive word play and verbal jousting around the definitions of what their objects or pictures did or didn't mean. The following text shows how those exchanges bordered on a kind of theater of the absurd.

Sabrina: *(sharing a stuffed toy)* This is my dog and I had it a very long time, and I sleeped with it in my bed, and my daddy gave it to me. Questions or comments.
Dan: *(very seriously)* It isn't a pet. I mean, it isn't a dog, it's a cat.
Sabrina: *(looking carefully at the toy, and shaking her head)* No, it's a dog. It has a tail. See! *(points to the tail)*
Dan: *(smiling and shaking his head)* No, it's a cat. It really is.

SABRINA: *(staring firmly at Dan and shaking her head in the negative)*
It's a dog.

DAN: *(looking around at the audience, which is starting to smile at the
exchange)* Um. *(turning his gaze back at Sabrina and raising his eye-
brows)* It's not a dog. It's a cat . . . *(pauses for effect)* And I like it.

CLARA: It's a dog, Dan.

BOBBIE: Yeah, Dan, it really is a dog. You just *think* it's a cat.

THOMAS: I like it a lot. How long have you had it, 'cause it looks
pretty old.

SABRINA: Thank you. Well, my dad got it at the store.

CLIFF: Sabrina, he asked how long you had it.

SABRINA: Well, he doesn't have any teeth.

JUSTIN: Where are his teeth? Is his mouth closed?

CLIFF: Does a robot control it?

SABRINA: No. There's no robot. It's not a robot! Silly!

LEILA: How long have you had that stuffed animal puppy?

SABRINA: For long, long, long, long, long.

GEORGE: *(hands placed sincerely across his chest)* I know it's a dog.

SABRINA: Thank you.

DAN: *(smiling slyly)* Dogs and cats both have tails, and all cats sometimes are black. And they have, they're like that. *(pointing to the
toy)* Those are what cats look like. Well, it is a cat.

SABRINA: *(quite calmly)* No, it's a dog. (Sharing Time, December 17)

"CARNIVAL" IN THE STYLE OF KINDERGARTEN

Sessions like this one continued and soon expanded to include all the children in the class as both initiators and interactive audience members. By
May, many children who had been silent and self-conscious during more
spontaneous performances were improvising songs and orchestrating
dances and musical events. That signaled to me that the children had made
a movement toward understanding their roles as co-performers as well as
realizing the social benefits of the authoring process and, further, that they
were comfortable taking the risks that those kinds of performances
required. Both audience members and the sharing child created texts as
they went along, becoming mutually aware of both the pace of the
exchanges and the uses of hyperbole, understatement, humor, and audience response.

Often these sessions ended with a breakdown of order and general hilarity that I could not control. My response to that loss of control was not teacherly in that I didn't try to wrest it back. Because I wanted these children to be more active in the development of the public discourse of the classroom, I knew that using my authority to control the social outcome of the authoring process would derail their efforts. And to be quite honest, a part of me liked the loss of control; it was funny and spontaneous and the end result was a kind of joyfulness that deepened the links in our community and expanded the children's expressive repertoires.

Readers of Bakhtin (1984) will recognize the elements of carnival in this description. Although my students were creating a carnival atmosphere in the style of kindergarten, the issues that surround carnival as a public event were obviously present in their work. Many of their exchanges used parody to propel them forward into laughter and disorder. In creating space for the idea of authoring, I was sanctioning what some researchers have characterized as a potentially dangerous textual space where children's meanings and intentions as authors can be destructive (Lensmire, 1994, 1997; Swaim, 1998, 2002). As control of the public discourse continually shifted from child to child through the authoring process, the established authority in the classroom—in this case, that of the teacher—was purposefully undermined, making the dynamic both exciting and risky.

What I learned from those occasions, and what I have observed in this research, is that dynamic, dialogic communities cannot be created unless I, as a teacher, embrace the authoring process and all it risks. The process of creating improvised, collaborative texts served as a gateway to the development of my students' public identities as individuals who influenced the thinking, feeling, and imaginative worlds of their peers. In essence, we were creating a "thought community" (Fleck, 1979; John-Steiner, 2000; John-Steiner & Meehan, 1999). As control over the public discourse moved from child-to-child to teacher-to-child and back again, every member of the community participated in constructing, critiquing, and reflecting on the texts being created.

In Chapter 4, I asked what it would take for any of us to begin to master subjects that were undoable. I would answer now that it takes a learning environment where there are opportunities to engage in authoring and the performances necessary for creating literate identities, with students and teacher acting as imaginative, engaged co-authors.

PART III

Imagination in the Real World

FRAME

"Breakdown at Marty's Quik Stop"

Thursday morning, gassing up the "new" used car in Danville, Vermont, my husband, Dave, fills the Peugeot, remarking as he does so that the dealer told him he doesn't have to use Super Unleaded. I nod, happy to have a car that goes and doesn't grind in gear, a car whose muffler is silent, whose body isn't pitted with rust. Dave gets in the driver's seat, turns the starter, and all the lights and buzzers go on, but the car does not start. He tries again, then a third time. Five minutes later we are sitting glumly in the same spot wondering where in this god forsaken-piece of the Northeast Kingdom we are going to find a Peugeot dealer whose computer can diagnose our problem.

Dave walks into Marty's Quik Stop to find a pay phone and returns with the owner of the store, who pops the hood and peers inside. He's wearing a butcher's apron, and I wonder if he's also a mechanic. He and Dave stare purposefully into the engine, poking here and there as men do (oh, I catch myself here, some women, too, although not me; that's a huge gap in my education), but they both rise up out of the hood silent.

117

Just then, a crumpled-up Vega pulls in with three passengers: two men and a child in the back seat. The driver hops out to pump gas. He exchanges a greeting with the butcher and, on seeing the opened hood, he jumps into action. He is thirtyish, muscular, and redheaded with a hint of balding. He wears wire-rim glasses that seem uncharacteristic when coupled with the rumpled Vega, faded T-shirt and jeans, and rolled-up sleeves that show promising biceps. As Dave describes our problem, he literally jumps into the engine cavity, perching on the edge of the opened hood, then takes off his glasses—"to see better"—puts his ear to the engine, pokes and prods. The butcher saunters off, apparently feeling he's been relieved.

The Vega is pulled to our side by the second man, and as he jumps out and joins us, I realize he's a teenager, thin and lanky, his hair uncombed. He stands to the side of the engine watching carefully as his companion continues to poke and prod while also explaining to Dave that this is that and that is this, and here's the black box like he put on his Bimmer—"$350 bucks, can you believe it for a computer chip?" I am feeling somehow slightly better. He's got Dave busy trying the starter. The teenager is handing him screwdrivers. He's using two to check the starter. I am getting an inkling that I am seeing something unusual happening in front of me, something I can recognize but not quite put my finger on. I peer into the engine with my usual fog of total ignorance. Everything looks shiny and OK to me. Nothing is anything. I just want the car to go. The redhead continues to poke and put his ear to different parts of the car. He crawls underneath and almost gets run over as the car rolls toward him, but he's quick, springs up, and muses out loud about the external fuse box. The child, also a redhead, plays quietly in the back seat of the Vega.

Dave looks puzzled and discouraged, but this lone ranger of mechanics hops into the driver's seat with one of his screwdrivers, pops out a fuse box, exclaiming, "God Almighty, would you look at that technology!" and fiddles with the circuit breaker. Back to the engine he goes, continuing his running lesson on the parts of the Peugeot—chattering to Dave about F-16's, which he apparently repairs. This is getting more interesting. Four of us look deeply into the engine as he works over the car, eliminating each possible problem. He asks Dave to try the starter one more time. I am not confident. Dave turns the key . . . and damn, the thing goes!

The Lone Ranger stands up and smiles. The kid and I look incredu-
lously at each other, shaking our heads. Dave sighs deeply. I peer into
the engine again and marvel out loud at the spectacle we have just
witnessed. "Boy, that was amazing," I say to the kid.

"I know," he answers with awe in his voice. "He's a certified
mechanic." I nod, and we are both humbled in the face of the deep
mechanical intelligence we have just witnessed.

"I'm still learning," the boy says softly.

This journal entry brings to our attention a fine example of literacy *in the
world*. We see the master, the apprentice, and uninitiated observers participating in the solution of a real-life problem. What was most striking to me
was the combination of curiosity and deep knowledge that the mechanic
brought to the problem. His solution seemed magical to me as an outsider,
but his teenage apprentice seemed to understand that although what we had
observed was indeed remarkable, that level of expertise might be possible
for him.

When this was written, I was not far along in my study of imagination.
I had not begun to generalize about how what I was observing as a teacher
of children related to the outside world and achievement beyond school.
This observation, though, points to the role imagination plays in attaining
a high level of functioning in the world of work. As I watched, I saw many
aspects of imagination operating simultaneously: wonder, curiosity, creativity, experimentation, problem solving, intuition—all these capacities
joined with deep knowledge of a field to produce a high level of literacy
(and, I suspect, of achievement). My record of this incident offers a frame
through which to consider how imagination might reshape our understanding of the purposes and outcomes of schooling. What kind of world-
view are we shaping in the classroom? Are we preparing our students to
meet their present and future lives with wonder, curiosity, creativity, experimentation, and courage in the face of the unknown? What changes might
occur in the classroom, and in the world, if imagination were put at the center of teaching and learning?

CHAPTER 7

Imagining a Different World: Sociocultural Literacy

> I take humanness, and the valuing of humanness, as starting place for education—and for society. . . . I offer humanness as widely distributed capacity, as active making, as value, as resource, as scale, as process, and as responsibility. (Carini, 2001, p. 1)

In the last chapter, we saw the way in which the process of authoring reshapes the patterns of interaction in the classroom. Roles shift: Students and teacher take risks by opening up the imaginative space. In this chapter, I will discuss some of the implications for building rich classroom communities that result when "open" imaginative space are part of a classroom's pedagogical design. I propose that this open space promotes a different kind of literate behavior that is as important as those we seek in academic subjects—one that might be called a sociocultural literacy.

CLASSROOMS AS SITES OF CULTURAL CONTACT

In her introduction to the second edition of *Classroom Discourse*, Courtney Cazden (2001) writes about the "new basic skills" students graduating in the 21st century will need. Among them, she lists "the ability to work in groups with persons of various backgrounds" (p. 5), and she points out:

> Learning different patterns of language use . . . involves changing more than words alone. It entails taking on new roles, and the new identities they express—for students as well as teachers. (p. 6)

As an early childhood teacher, I have often experienced this kind of change, but it is difficult to explicitly name what this kind of change means in my classroom. Other recent movements in education have attempted to describe and/or conceptualize this kind of work. *Emancipatory literacy* (Friere, 1972; Friere & Macedo, 1987), *critical literacy, the caring curriculum* (Noddings, 1992), *You can't say you can't play* (Paley, 1993), and *multicultural education* are a few terms and phrases that immediately come to mind. Yet there is a deeper kind of experience that I want to name here, one that encompasses all the goals of such projects but is rooted in the deep structure of classroom life.

Teaching young children forces me to think in a different way about the project of building social and cultural understanding with, and among, my students. For me, activism emerges from the context of our daily life in the classroom; it is stitched back onto my students' efforts to be literate through the project of humanism. We resist injustice and are tolerant, respectful, and caring because, as Carini (2001) proposes, we celebrate our "humanness" in all its variety and depth. A focus on humanness, what Paul Nash (1966) and others in the 1960s and 1970s called "humanistic education," ought to be at the center of our teaching and our learning. As such, it requires us to be aware of how we, as "cultural beings ... critique, challenge, resist, create, and recreate our social worlds" (Schwartz, 1995, p. 638).

Classrooms today are potentially rich sites of cultural contact; they are "La Frontera, The Borderlands" (Anzaldua, 1987), and they offer many opportunities for students to understand plurality (Friere & Macedo, 1987). Gloria Anzaldua (1987) defines the borderlands as a place where:

> two or more cultures edge each other, where people of different races occupy the same territory, where under, lower, middle and upper classes touch, where the space between two individuals shrinks with intimacy. (p. i)

She points out that the exploration and development of self in the context of meeting those who are different is part of growth and change:

> Living on borders and in margins, keeping intact one's shifting and multiple identity and integrity, is like trying to swim in a new element, an alien element. There is an exhilaration in being a participant in the further evolution of humankind, in being "worked" on. ... Certain "faculties" ... in every border resident ... and dormant areas of consciousness are being activated, awakened. (p. i)

Anzaldua's reference to the "exhilaration" one feels when participating in the development of human understanding very much captures why I find the daily process of building a classroom community so provocative. I am excited, for myself and my students, by the process. I know the ways in which I have grown and am "worked on" through it, and, through my research, I have been able to document how that happens for my students.

SOCIOCULTURAL LITERACY IN A CLASS OF DIVERSE LEARNERS

The discourse of sociocultural literacy, like that of all other literacies, requires students and teachers to build new identities:

> identities that are not empty vehicles for the production of sameness, for the reproduction of racial authenticity and purity, but identities that can enable us to cross borders and experience different cultural locations. (Estrada & McClaren, 1993, p. 29)

In this case, what is under construction is human understanding. This is not, in my opinion, a separate pedagogical agenda that can be written into lesson plans. Rather, it is ongoing, permeating all of classroom life. As I have emphasized in earlier chapters, the process of becoming literate is both personal and social. Developing a sociocultural literacy, therefore, cannot be separated from the work of encountering new texts, ideas, ideologies, languages, and forms of expression. It is actualized in the public forums of classrooms and school; it asks the teacher to take on a different pedagogical tone within a community of practice. It requires the work of imagination to come to fruition.

This chapter returns to the work of the first-grade children described in Chapter 3 to illustrate the changes I have observed when the celebration of humanness and the construction of sociocultural understanding are the supports upon which a thought community is built. I have chosen this class because they were a diverse, dynamic group of learners, but they were not naturally respectful and harmonious. The class included a representative cross-section of the urban community in which they lived: five racial groups (Asian, European American, African American, Hispanic, Native American), diverse first-language backgrounds (English, Spanish, Russian, Czech, Chinese, Japanese, Italian); a range of socioeconomic levels (families in public housing, blue-collar families, graduate students, artists, professionals, college professors); different family structures (single parent on public assistance, single working parent, one parent at home and one in the work force, two working parents, two working parents with live-in domestic help); varied political status (U.S. citizens, new immigrants, nationals from other countries); and different religious affiliations (Protestant, Catholic, Jewish, Buddhist, Native American). The descriptions that follow document the development of the children's relationships as a class over time. Within that description I focus attention on one child, Donaldo, in order to illustrate how these children developed a broader understanding of "humanness" through the practice of community building.

Building Community from Diversity

> SOPHIA: *(sharing a bird's nest she found in Italy)* Oh, if it was a Italian bird, and it laid Italian eggs, then if I brought the eggs to this country, and they hatched it might not work because they'd live in the wrong place . . . They'd probably only speak Italian. (Sharing Time, September 21)

Here, approximately 2 weeks into the schoolyear in my first record of sharing time, Sophia delivered these lines completely pokerfaced, and, as she finished, carefully scanned her audience to see if any of them got the joke. No one—except Nat, Sarah, and me—had.

As the reader will recall, this class was extraordinarily creative and imaginative. They were not, however, all operating at the same level of sophistication in their oral expression. Some, such as Sophia and Nat, had sophisticated understandings of irony and humor. Others were still thrilled with bathroom jokes. They were also diverse as learners. Betty and Sasha were early readers and writers; Nat could read at the fourth-grade level, multiply, and divide; some children were still learning the alphabet and how to count. A few, such as Fuyuka, couldn't speak English but could read and write in their native language. Some found school to be very threatening. Sonny, for example, was always discouraged and pessimistic before he even began a task and regularly threw tantrums when he felt threatened by a new activity.

Most of the children were very social, loving to talk and perform with their friends, but few were aware of the effects of their behavior. There were varying levels of insensitivity toward the feelings of others, some resulting from ignorance, some from pride, and some from prejudice. Here, for example, is an excerpt from fieldnotes recorded during a quiet reading time.

Sonny, sitting with Nat, is working on a predictable book we've read several times. He says, rather proudly, to Nat, "Hey, I'm already on page 5, Nat!"

Nat replies, rather smugly, "Well, I've already finished that and now I am reading a chapter book." Needless to say, Sonny was a bit upset to hear that reply. (Fieldnotes, October 24, taken by Sarah)

There were a few children, such as Emily, who were quite introverted and preferred not to socialize with friends. Jamilla, who was overweight and struggled with the teasing of the boys and a few of the girls in the class, spent time alone to avoid being hurt but did not hesitate to taunt others when their weaknesses showed. There were power struggles. Brian and Peter immediately locked horns in early September over who was smarter. Some struggled with my authority. Sasha was unable to accept my decisions, meeting every activity I initiated with the question "Why?" and a series of objections to the plans. Yet, in spite of their differences, this class began to work together enthusiastically in two different parts of the day: sharing time and the afternoon period when they chose different expressive activities. I would propose that what they achieved as a community resulted, in part, from the imaginative spaces I opened up in order to study how they worked with imagination.

Donaldo

Descanso

There are no front teeth
but not because the tooth fairy came.
How they were lost is a mystery his mother won't tell.
Still, the smile is enormous
bigger than my heart can comprehend
and he gives it freely.

My six year old Latin lover, he is not faithful—
he could charm birds out of trees—
but there are a few things missing besides those teeth
like shoes that fit, a coat in winter, his alphabet
numbers, colors, shapes.
And there is the absence of a settled grammar

> his lives somewhere between English and Spanish.
> Oh, we do scramble for him!
> A legion of teachers rowing towards the shore
> as the current of his life pulls him away.
> Then one day he is gone
> another of America's Disappeared.
>
> The winter sky is hard and grey.
> Birds cannot sing.

I wrote this poem about Donaldo as a first attempt to reconcile the contradictions of Donaldo's life with us in school and my sorrow at his loss. In March Donaldo dropped out of sight. One day Donaldo was a living, vibrant presence in our classroom; the next, he seemed to have vanished. Looking back on it now, I see that I missed something. It was true that the teachers who worked with him devoted a tremendous amount of energy trying to shore him up so that he could catch up with his peers academically, and it was true that the degree of charm and openness he had for the world was almost heartbreaking in the joy it transferred to everyone he encountered on a daily basis. But the poem omitted an important kind of support that Donaldo received, and offered, each day. That was the work he and the other children in the classroom did to forge new kinds of relationships and social understandings.

Donaldo entered first grade with few academic skills and little English but a great deal of enthusiasm. In early September he could not recognize his letters, colors, numerals, shapes; could not sing the alphabet, count to 5, or copy simple patterns with beads. Lacking these skills, however, did not stop him from participating creatively in our daily activities. One day, for example, when we were counting the children in the class, Donaldo counted the days on the calendar as a way of figuring out the number of children. By the third week in September, though, he had learned to count to 10, and, because he loved singing and making up new songs (as we've seen in Chapter 6), he would sing the alphabet song throughout the day. But above all else, what Donaldo enjoyed was interacting with other children, and his sunny outlook on life, paired with a natural affability, endeared him to them. From the beginning, they readily invited him to work and play with them, encouraging him to join them in blocks and drama even though at first he could not join in their conversations.

Sharing Time

Donaldo did not share until early November. Up until that time, he had watched and listened carefully as his classmates shared, but the limitations of his spoken English prevented him from participating during questions or comments (the exchange that followed each child's presentation). On November 13, however, he got in the sharing chair holding a shoe box, opened it with a big smile on his face, and began to pull out coupons he had cut out from the newspaper and some drawings of his own done on scraps of lined paper. The pictures and drawings included a Christmas tree, a wreath, a picture frame, and other pictures of ribbon, ornaments, and so on.

At first, as he started showing the pictures without any accompanying explanation, some children were puzzled and said so. When that kind of talk began, though, Betty quickly said, in her curt authoritative way, "This is Donaldo's sharing time—be quiet," and the class quieted down. From that point on, each time he showed a new picture, the children in the audience clapped. As he finished, he asked for "questions and comments." The questions that followed were specific: "Where'd you get the pictures? Did you make Thanksgiving ones? How did you make the pictures?" His answers were brief, but he made an attempt to explain how he had used pencil and crayons for the drawings.

What was immediately striking to me as I watched was that following Betty's intervention, the class was working hard to scaffold Donaldo into sharing time as a communal activity, not caring that he was sharing newspaper coupons and scraps of paper. Betty's intervention made it clear that it was the audience's role to pay attention and figure out what Donaldo was doing. I realized from that exchange that there were some children who understood Donaldo's predicament and were careful to be respectful of him. More surprising, though, was the way the entire group of children fell in line and spontaneously rewarded his efforts.

A week later, Donaldo shared again. This time he brought in an envelope full of papers. Different letters of the alphabet were written on each piece of paper. He couldn't explain much about what he had done, but he asked again for questions and comments. About 10 hands shot up. Again, the questions were specific, requiring only one-word answers. One that came at the end asked how he had made the letters.

> **DONALDO:** I thought, then I wrote *(reciting these slowly and deliberately)* A, B, C, D, E, F, G . . .

He stopped, unable to remember the rest of the letters, but the class immediately joined into the recitation, and Jamilla started to sing the ABC song, which he so loved. Donaldo joined back into the song, but faltered again at "L, M, N, O, P." At this, Sonny leaned close to him and coached him softly: "M, N, O, P." Donaldo went back, repeated what Sonny had said, and then finished the song with the class.

Small Steps

> Karen asks Sasha if she needs to "get in" during science talk (meaning join in on the conversation). Donaldo, who is sitting next to Sasha, moves over on the rug to make room so that Sasha could physically move in closer to the group. Sasha looks at him like he's crazy, then says "Ohhhh," as she figures out why he moved over. She whispers to him, "No, Karen means, do I want to talk?" Donaldo looks over at me, smiles, and shrugs his shoulders. (Fieldnotes, Science Talk, November 29, taken by Sarah)

> Donaldo phrases a correct question to Sarah as a child shares, "What is that thing in her hand?" (Sharing Time, December 1)

> **DONALDO:** *(sharing a picture he drew)* This is a house. These are the windows. And this is the garage.
>
> [This text is quite coherent and easy to understand.]
>
> **QUESTION:** Why is there no door?
> **DONALDO:** I didn't have room. (Sharing Time, December 4)

As Sarah and I tracked Donaldo's work in class, we began to see small changes in his understanding and use of English and in his academic skills. During the week of December 12, Donaldo had been absent the first day of the week and came in saying, "I was sick with a stomach." In the morning, as the children drew in their art journals, he was singing his own version of "Jingle Bells" and carrying on with great joy with Peter and Brian as they all drew together:

> **DONALDO:** Question! Who loves dinner?

This phrase followed upon a series of questions Brian had asked that began with, "Who loves . . . ?" Donaldo, though, added the exclamation each time: "Question!"

A bit later in the morning meeting, he read without hesitation the names of the children who were absent and counted how many children were buying lunch and how many had brought lunch. It was astonishing to see this when I considered what he had been able to do when he entered school in September. Two days later, it was Donaldo's turn to read the daily schedule:

> Donaldo's day to read the chart. He is getting through it by sheer intelligence, using his memory of repetitions in our daily schedule. The children around him are giving him quiet cues using first sounds in the words and he guesses, correctly, what the words are, using his knowledge of what activity might begin with that sound. He comes to the word *gym*, and I've left out the *G* at the beginning, which he is supposed to fill in. He says, "G," but doesn't know how to write the letter. He turns to the class for help. All the boys in the class start showing him how to write a *G* in the air. Three boys are saying out loud, "I'll show you," as they make the *G*'s in the air. Donaldo is looking at each of them, trying to sort out these signals. Then he exclaims, "Wait a minute! Wait a minute! I know! Is this it?" and he makes a *G* in the air correctly, and the children say "Yeah!"
>
> "I *knew* it!" he says and pumps his arms a bit in triumph as athletes do when they've scored. Then he smiles his absolutely charming toothless smile, raises his eyebrows, lifts the marker dramatically, turns backs to the chart, and writes a *G*. We are all very happy. (Fieldnotes, December 12)

Incidents such as this demonstrated for me how important the class's interactions with Donaldo were for his overall development as a learner and for their sense of solidarity with him. The reality of the situation was that some of the children who were helping him were not much ahead of him academically. When any one of them took a turn reading the chart, a similar scenario would often occur. Donaldo's case, though, demonstrates the skill with which they worked with his language and cultural differences and his skill in responding intelligently and gracefully.

Developing Sharing-Time Language

In late January I asked the children to switch from showing objects for sharing to telling something without an object as a prop. This represented a great challenge for all students, especially for second-language learners such as Donaldo, but he was enthusiastic:

> **DONALDO:** I saw a strange street. All the fire trucks on the side of the street. My sister, and my mom, and my baby saw it. And the cops run, and there was a fire, and the people run out. And they don't have no food. And they go to the hospital. *(He continues on with what I think is a description of how a fire truck works.)* They put a water in the fire so they be out. They need to go home cause they have no home. So the cops give them a home.
>
> **QUESTION:** Where did it happen?
>
> **DONALDO:** That's a *real* question. It happened in Brookline. (Sharing Time, January 29)

Building Imaginary Worlds Through Stories

As with other classes I had taught over the years, this class quickly transitioned from telling true stories to building "fake" stories that emphasized friendships but also expressed in their plots the natural social tensions that are present in any community (Gallas, 1994, 1998). (Note that my students, not I, introduced the term *fake* to describe their stories.) Storytellers such as Sophia, Jamilla, Nat, and Barbara regaled the class with bizarre and creative story lines, sometimes using shock value to grab their audience's attention. All the children developed imaginative stories that placed one another in desirable or undesirable predicaments. Exchanges during questions or comments were energetic and sometimes contentious, as certain children took exception to their characterizations by the storytellers or objected to too much violence—or romantic allusions by the girls. The class as a whole developed an honest and direct way of giving and responding to feedback. It was during sharing time that these students developed their ability to work together and reasonably negotiate their differences through the medium of their narrative imaginations.

DEVELOPING COLLABORATIVE TEXTS:
FAKE STORIES

The children's stories were often co-constructed; that is, the storyteller would take or seek guidance and ideas from audience members. An example of one such story, told by Sasha in her first attempt at a fake story, gives the flavor of the kinds of exchanges that resulted as the audience participated.

> SASHA: I've never ever ever done a fake story.
> SOPHIA: Just try it.
> SASHA: I don't know how to start.
> SOPHIA: Say, "Once upon a time."
> SASHA: OK. Once upon a time.
>
> [She starts, then stops, and then starts again. The story that develops is a class trip to Candyland. The children really like the idea.]
>
> BARBARA: I want to be in it!
> SASHA: They went in the house and in the house lived a little girl named Barbara.
>
> [There is a lot of audience prompting and funneling of ideas. She stops and confers with her audience about whether the school was candy.]
>
> SASHA: Of course, it was in Candyland.
>
> [Then a discussion ensues about the contents of the school. Someone asks, "Were the pens licorice? Black licorice?"]
>
> SASHA: Don't talk to me about black licorice. I hate it. But my mother is crazy for black and red licorice! And the monkey bars were chocolate!

This exchange is notable because it shows Sasha engaged in what, for her, was an important developmental task: trying something she considered to be risky and hard. Yet here she feels comfortable enough to get up in front of the class and admit that she was unsure of herself. She asks for help in the beginning and receives it immediately from Sophia, who is an adept storyteller. In fact, as I observed the children share from day to day, I saw that many of them asked for and accepted help when they needed it. This was clearly a protocol that the children understood and used for their own benefit, and Donaldo was no exception.

Donaldo was enchanted by these stories and often bid to be in them as the story unfolded. His first story, told in February, was modeled on his observations of the key elements of many of the stories that he had heard, with one misinterpretation of a device used in those stories. In many of the stories, the storyteller would create mishaps for the characters, who were usually their closest friends, but would also include him- or herself as a victim of the mishap. This generally made the bad situation that other children, as characters, had fictionally been placed in acceptable, because the storyteller was also at a disadvantage. In the story that follows, however, Donaldo used the formula of including friends and food fights (which were popular with the boys, Jamilla, Sophia, and Barbara) but misused the bad situation. That created a problem for his audience, which they clearly conveyed to him by both their comments and their physical responses. (Note in the text how I cued him to rectify the situation, which he tried to do but did not succeed in entirely.)

DONALDO: Once upon a time was five little boys. Brian was piece of pie. Brian running around, running around and taking off his hair. Next is Nat, Nateroni, and he was running around on a bike. And Chinua, putting a pizza in his face. This was Peter. He be a fat little pig.

PETER: I don't think that's funny.

KAREN: Donaldo, I think you better do something to yourself.

DONALDO: Uh, Brian, Peter, Chinua, Nat, and me, we all pigs. All the pigs go in the door and we can't fit in the door! We can't put our fat little in the door. Except for Brian. He got stuck.

(Brian looks like he's going to cry.)

In this sharing session, Donaldo had clearly not understood all the ground rules of telling stories that included friends. Although he had made an attempt to correct his early mistake, the later reference to Brian getting stuck was hurtful. Brian, whom Donaldo loved and admired, was a bit husky, and he was sensitive about that. Donaldo had obviously noticed Brian's somatotype and felt, mistakenly, that it could be referenced in his story.

From stories that followed, though, it appears he had gotten the message. By March, the class had increasingly moved toward telling stories that included everyone, although they did not use everyone's name, often just implying that the story was about the whole class by using the words *they* or *we* or *the class*. For example, Brian, in opening "a fake story about birthday land," issued an invitation to his audience, "Everybody who's had a birthday can come." Prior to that time, many storytellers had included only a few friends in their stories as characters. What I observed in those cases was that their audience stopped listening when the action didn't include them. Apparently, the storytellers also made the same observation because the incidence of exclusive stories diminished over time.

In Donaldo's stories from March, which were still limited because of his developing vocabulary and syntax, he attempted to include all the boys and to appeal to the class's interests. The following brief story shows what he had understood:

> **DONALDO:** This is a fake story. And this is *(counts the boys in the class)* six, no seven little boys. Now, once upon a time, it is, um, it was, well, his name is Tommy. And Tommy eat all the ice cream. Nobody had some. Tommy run away. Well, Sonny turn [??] into Tommy.
> **DONALDO:** Questions or comments.
> **SOPHIA:** Did Sophia come and chase Tommy all the way to heaven around the neighborhood?
> **DONALDO:** No.
> **SOPHIA:** Did I follow him?
> **DONALDO:** Yes.

Here Donaldo attempted to include all the boys, although he named only Tommy and Sonny. When Sophia expressed her desire to be included in the story, he acquiesced, putting her in as a minor part of the action, knowing, as did the rest of the children, that Sophia's romantic pursuit of Tommy in her stories was embarrassing to Tommy. So Donaldo, although struggling with language and the telling of the story, was not struggling with the social implications of his words. He had a clear understanding at this point of the social dynamics of the classroom.

As time passed, the children in the audience began to find out that if they wanted to be included in a story, and weren't, they should ask to be. Donaldo also took up this strategy. For example, Sonny told a story in early March that began with only himself as a character:

> **SONNY:** *(musing to himself and the audience)* Hmm. True or fake? What is this? I had a dream, about dinosaurs chasing me.

[As he's telling the dream, Chinua interrupts.]

CHINUA: How many boys does it have?

SONNY: Hmm. [He names all the boys in the class and continues with the story, but Chinua bids to be included in more parts and Sonny accommodates him.]

DONALDO: And how about me?

SONNY: Donaldo, him, he almost fell off the tail. *(Tommy is energetically pointing to himself.)* And let's see what Tommy did.

ESTABLISHING THE GROUNDWORK FOR SOCIOCULTURAL LITERACY

What I saw, when I looked at this data within the framework of sociocultural literacy, was that the endeavor of creating a cohesive, respectful learning community is not a haphazard process, but it is also not something that can be programmed by the teacher. In the past, when I saw that a child did not fit into the mainstream of classroom life, I believed it was my responsibility to orchestrate opportunities that would pull him or her into the social network of the class. I am sure that we have all had students whose difference resulted in exclusion and even provoked cruelty in some children. In those cases, it is natural for us to act as matchmakers in friendships or as advocates for the excluded child. Our motives in these cases are clearly benevolent, but, as I have learned more about imagination and about literacy, my perspective on how sociocultural awareness grows and supports the development of a healthy community has changed.

Viewing the classroom from a more open, watchful position has helped me become acutely aware that it is not my responsibility alone to pull a student like Donaldo into the mainstream of classroom life and, thus, make him fit into a preexisting kind of social reality that I have established. Rather, it is *our* responsibility as community members to create the sociocultural mainstream of the classroom from the ground up each and every year. This kind of work forces everyone to begin to modify their behavior and their thinking, to relate to one another as people they are interested in knowing better, people who are different but also intriguing, people in whom they find joy, laughter, and sorrow, rather than people who can't speak English or speak it too fast, or who are poor or rich, or whose skin is a different color, or whose behavior is odd.

Our work in this class was about developing a community in which anyone could participate with safety, and, although I consciously took a role in creating that kind of safety, some of my students also brought that ethic with them to school. Safety and respect for others were values we developed together as we worked in the open imaginative spaces of sharing time and our afternoon work periods. It was ongoing work from September through March, when Donaldo left us. And even after he was gone, the lessons we had learned from him and with him about language, culture, belonging, and difference remained. Sharing time continued without Donaldo—but not without reference to him. We continued to debate, co-create, contest, and perform, but our ability to do so respectfully was greater because we had met, worked, loved, and played with Donaldo in a genuine and honest way. This kind of early sociocultural work changed the way these young children related to one another and the kinds of possible worlds they imagined themselves into. It is also important to say here that this kind of work changed me and the possible worlds I imagine for myself and the children I teach. Although most of the transcripts in this chapter—and, indeed, in this book—highlight only my students' voices, in fact, I was at all times a co-actor in every exchange. I sat in the sharing-time sessions as a member of the audience, and sometimes I was a performer. I reacted with dismay and joy when something alarmed or delighted me. In all cases, I was attempting with my students to be fully present in body, mind, and spirit in this "apprenticeship" experience.

Our work together leads me to wonder what would happen if all children in all parts of the world had the opportunity to explore, on a daily basis, what it means to be human in the midst of diversity. How might the world be different if children throughout their schooling were allowed to take time each day to create texts about themselves in relationship with others, to debate and contest through those texts how they were being perceived and positioned, to understand through struggle what the process of building an inclusive, respectful social order looks and feels like?

CHAPTER 8

Reclaiming, Renaming, Reimagining the Classroom

> Sophia enters the classroom, walks straight up to me as I stand by my desk speaking with a parent and says, quite seriously and without a greeting, "Karen, here's what I want to know. Where do I go when I'm dead? Because I don't want to go just anywhere, you know. I don't want to end up in a pile of garbage at the dump. I'd rather be a jelly-bean on the top of a giant hill of jellybeans. And I need to know. So you have to tell me right now. Where do I go?" She stops, stares, and there is no trace of the usual Sophia smile and the twinkle in her eye. Well, I am speechless. (Fieldnotes, October 2)

Each day in every classroom across this country moments like this one with Sophia occur. Usually these moments evaporate and are lost to teachers as ways of making sense of our teaching lives, both for ourselves and for others. I want to witness these moments, to have them fill me up so that I can live *in them*. In my interactions with students, I try to create a climate where those kinds of thoughts will be made public, because I believe they have important implications, not just for the development of our community but also for my ability to understand my students and, therefore, to teach them better.

I knew that morning that Sophia's words had profound meaning and importance for her as a student in my class and for me as her teacher. But at the moment of that event, the vitality of the classroom closed in around us. Other children arrived and parents, too, all making bids for my attention. Sophia continued her tirade as she walked into the meeting area to greet our bunny. Another parent who had heard the exchange wondered out loud what *I, I,* would tell her. I wondered how to get out of telling her anything. The birds squawked for their morning treat, visions of the separation of church and state popped into my head, and I just milled around, unnerved by her question on both an inquisitive, ethnographic level, and on a personal one: Where, indeed, do we go when we die? I didn't really want to go just anywhere either.

TEACHING AS ETHNOGRAPHY

Each classroom in this country and in the world, like mine, is a unique, living community. Students and teachers arrive with a set of cultural practices and beliefs about schooling and each of the subjects that will be studied. Over time, a class and a teacher work together, and their practices and beliefs begin to amalgamate and modify. As I pointed out in Chapter 7, in a classroom where open spaces are created for imaginative discourse and action, there is no preestablished, predictable "mainstream" of thought and action to which students must conform to fit in. The mainstream that is created comes from the process of building a self-conscious thought community that acknowledges, and reflects on, the texts created by students and teachers alike. As such, there is always the possibility that ideas and concerns, such as the one Sophia introduced on that day in October, can surface.

As a teacher in such a community, I know that every event influences and changes the classroom, creating a constantly evolving, newly imagined cultural system. In this chapter, I first explore how the process of ethnography enables teachers and students to inquire into classroom culture and practice. I follow that exploration with a description of how that process of inquiry can lead to a deep shift in the ways that teachers and students approach instruction, learning, and curriculum—*an imaginative revisioning of the classroom through which we reclaim, rename, and reimagine teaching and learning.* Let me begin by returning to Sophia—and death.

Violet the Bunny

> Violet died Thursday morning after a short illness—8 years old. She ate her last banana on Tuesday. I came in and found her around 7:45 A.M. and was upset. News spread fast throughout the school. [See Figure 8.1.] (Fieldnotes, January 12)

FIGURE 8.1. "Violet died"

At the time that Sophia made her comment, Violet, our classroom bunny, was alive. A few months later, Violet passed away. She was 8 years old, an old bunny by any standard, and she had worked with many classes of children. So her death was traumatic and caused disruptions all over the school. On the morning of her death, I was doing damage control: trying to figure out what to do with a bunny carcass in a class full of children who were all demanding to see her (she was in a paper bag in my desk drawer); consoling parents, teachers, and other children who had visited Violet on a daily basis for years; taking attendance and lunch count; and so on.

As each of these events resolved themselves and the day settled down, I readied myself for the discussion of death and dying that I had always orchestrated following the death of a classroom pet. This is something that primary teachers are well prepared for and see as an important learning experience for children. But when I turned my attention back to the children, what did I find? They were all engaged in a self-initiated funerary project of turning Violet's cage into a shrine. They were cutting pieces of paper; writing poems and notes of good wishes on them; drawing portraits of Violet and pictures of their memories of her; wrapping those with ribbon, yarn, and even flowers and grasses they had picked in the schoolyard; and sticking them in the wire that enclosed her cage. Old signs that read "Violet's House" had been shrouded with pieces of fabric. The children had taken the stuffed bunnies from the drama center and perched them on top of her cage; they had woven extra ribbon, yarn, and flowers in the empty sections of wire mesh between the notes. Some children had put their morning snacks, especially those that Violet had enjoyed sharing with them (carrots, grapes, apples, and bananas), into the cage next to her food bowl. Later in the day, notes suspended on Popsicle sticks began to appear in the landscaping that bordered the playground. Never, to my knowledge, had a bunny been escorted out of this world with more care and solicitude. In the weeks and months following her death, Violet's cage remained untouched as a lasting shrine, and Violet began to enter our folklore. This account of the events following Violet's death is an example of the way in which a class of children constructs, with and without the teacher, a unique culture with its own set of rituals, folklore, history, and social conventions, making it ripe for ethnographic study.

Why Ethnography?

My interest in ethnography came out of my work with the Brookline Teacher Research Seminar, a group of teachers and researchers that began meeting in 1989 for the purposes of exploring issues of language and literacy. At first, our orientation was solely on inquiring into children's language. Gradually, however, the research practice of the teachers in the group moved toward ethnography, primarily because we became familiar with certain aspects of ethnography that immediately enriched our teaching even as they helped us begin to answer our research questions. Writing fieldnotes, audiotaping and videotaping classroom activities, collecting artifacts of classroom life, interviewing students to gain a better understanding of the ways in which they were perceiving classroom events—all of these were natural extensions of our teaching practice.

Early in our history we found that most of our inquiries into our teaching originated not with clear questions but with what we now call the "puzzling event" (Ballenger, 1999; Brookline Teacher Research Seminar, 2003; Gallas, 1994, 1998). That event was usually brought to the seminar in the form of an anecdote that would most commonly be told at the beginning of our weekly meeting, when we were putting out our snacks. Someone would say, "You know, something strange happened today, and I have no idea what it means or what I should do about it." From that would follow a request by other group members for a telling of the story, and thus a study would most likely begin, although the question behind the study probably would not become clear until much later. Our anecdotes were usually characterized by confusion and an inability to make the student's or students' behaviors fit into categories of meaning and explanation that had always worked before. I relayed my morning encounter with Sophia to the seminar later that day. It was pretty clear to me that I needed to make some sense of her words, but I couldn't say why. Thus, from the beginning, the heart of our research was motivated by surprise, wonder, and curiosity—all aspects of imaginative thought that helped us inquire more deeply into the meaning and implications of the event in question.

Now I'm pretty sure that most of my readers who are, or have been, teachers are quite familiar with this kind of situation. Anecdotes about a class are told on a daily basis by teachers to their colleagues, although sometimes with a different orientation. This kind of account can be either one of pure joy and surprise at something that children did or a complaint about the difficulty of teaching. Often a statement of difficulty is met by ideas about how to fix things or suggestions for different teaching strategies. What was interesting about the development of the puzzling event in the Brookline Seminar, though, was seminar members' reactions to the accounts of puzzling events. At no point did we try to fix the teacher's problem. *Instead, from the beginning of the seminar, we were encouraged to approach the problem as an open question—to view our students as making sense. Our work as teacher-researchers, therefore, was to figure out what that sense was.* As a result, we would encourage our colleagues to explore what the puzzling event embodied, to go back and inquire into the origins of the event and also into our own inability to understand it.

It is clear to me now that these puzzling events or points of confusion have parallels in ethnography. They are similar to what ethnographers call dissonant moments or frame clashes (Mehan, 1979)—points at which the ethnographer encounters an event that does not make sense within his or her cultural framework. In my opinion, if teachers study these dissonant moments as classroom ethnographers, we can look in a new way at these points of rupture and miscommunication. The practice of ethnography enables us to inspect them with an open imaginative point of view.

Literacy Narratives

I would like to propose that *students of any age who enter a classroom for the purposes of mastering a new subject bring with them "literacy narratives"* (Gallas & Smagorinsky, 2001)—*unique, usually unarticulated and unex-amined stories that represent cultural perspectives on learning, culled from home, the public world, and past experiences in classrooms.* Sometimes these narratives match school-based ways of thinking; sometimes not. All of these narratives embody a set of cultural understandings and cultural practices whose effect becomes yet another powerful subtextual dynamic in the class-room. As Halliday (1975) points out, "The reality that the child constructs is that of his culture and subculture, and the ways in which he learns to mean are also those of his culture and subculture" (1975, p. 143). The same can be said for the teacher: The reality we construct through our teaching is often determined by our culture and subculture.

So, for example, Denzel came in with a narrative about the uses of books: Books were for learning to read; they were tools for learning to decode sounds into words and for reading the words. In first grade, Denzel had learned that books were used to practice decoding words. He accepted that idea because it was congruent with his literacy narrative about the uses of books. Now, although I am certain Denzel did not listen to stories in first grade, his first-grade teacher did not insist upon that kind of participa-tion—so his literacy narrative about the uses of books and the purpose of reading remained unarticulated and unchallenged. But in my classroom I wanted him to be fully engaged in the read-aloud experience, and thus I challenged his assumptions. Although, like Denzel, I saw books as a tool for practicing reading, in my literacy narrative, books were also a source of in-formation about the world; they provided opportunities to enter new worlds of imagination and perception. Thus, it's not hard to understand why we encountered our blank space: Denzel could not see the relationship between story time and reading. Neither did he see nonfiction texts as resources for gathering information. There was a huge gap between his cultural understanding of books and mine.

Or we could say that his literacy narrative about books, from the perspective of both decoding and encoding, clashed with the literacy narrative my classroom practices embodied.

Denzel's Literacy Narrative

Book is for practicing reading.

Karen's Literacy Narrative

Book presents stories.
Book is a resource for information.
Book holds universal truths.
Book is for practicing reading.

Blank Spaces

I now believe that competing literacy narratives are behind many of the puzzling events and points of rupture I have encountered in my teaching. When a student and a teacher's literacy narratives clash, the result is the creation of a cognitive, behavioral, and expressive *blank space*. I use that term to describe times when students literally look blank and/or provide unsatisfactory responses to my repeated attempts to fix a breakdown in communication. To illustrate what I mean by the blank space that should be investigated, we can turn again to the breakdown in teaching that resulted when Denzel did not listen to stories. That blank space, which we both experienced, constituted a massive puzzling event that frustrated both Denzel and me for an entire schoolyear.

So there are two blank spaces that must be considered: The first is the teacher's, who in most of these puzzling moments has run out of answers and ideas for future interventions with students. The second is the student's. For the teacher, the teaching act does not draw an expected and purposeful response; for the student, the teacher's presentation of an activity does not fit into his or her beliefs about what constitutes learning. In other words, the student can't make sense of the teacher's instruction, and the teacher can't make sense of the student's response or lack thereof. *Inquiry into these points of rupture, these blank spaces, these dissonant moments, these puzzling events is where teaching as ethnography begins, precisely because the inquiry enables us to look freshly and imaginatively at an event—to make the familiar strange.*

Approaching a Text

My experience with Denzel has taught me that some ruptures and blank spaces in the learning process occur even before some students work with a particular text, whether it be a book, a math problem, or a dissection of a frog. In other words, even before a "reading" of a text begins, a student's presenting culture has a hand in what might be called *the approach to a text* (Gallas & Smagorinsky, 2001), the dance that takes place between a student and the text *before* the student will give the text a wholehearted reading— a reading in which he or she absolutely surrenders to the possibilities the text offers. Recall from Chapter 1 my reference to the "willing suspension of disbelief" (Coleridge, 1907, p. 6), the idea that each of us must give up our skeptical, detached view of the importance of an activity before we are able to fully participate in it. Much of my work on imagination, my fixation on trying to figure it out, has been focused on how to overcome that wall of detachment that I saw in Denzel and have seen in other students

Let me try to rephrase to be clearer: I believe there are three stages in the process of encountering a text of any kind. I call stage 1, which is the stage I am most concerned with, "the approach"; that is, will the potential reader choose to go beyond a utilitarian, "let's get through it to get the grade" view of the text? For example, as a student in college-level biology I would prepare the slides dutifully and follow the lab notes exactly, but when it came to making use of the slide to understand the meaning of what I was seeing and how it related to the purpose of the lab, I failed. To begin, many times I simply could not see what I was told I was supposed to see. Then, because of that basic perceptual problem, I gave up on the assigned task as a means of extending my understanding of biology. Because I couldn't even begin to work with the slide, I couldn't really "read" it. Therefore, I had no ability to respond to it or synthesize what it was telling me relative to the topic I was studying. I'd draw what I did see, and then leave it. In the real world of student–teacher interaction, the truth is that we can mandate a reading, but we cannot mandate engagement.

Assuming that the reader has made a decision to engage with the text, stage 2 includes the actual reading of the text, and stage 3 encompasses the reader's response to what has been read. In this scheme, however, I am stuck on stage 1, approach, because that seems to be my Waterloo. I can orchestrate the other two stages if the student has made an authentic approach, that is, if he or she believes the text has something to contribute to his or her own learning. But in the end, if a student doesn't approach a text, the "reading" won't happen in any effective way. Thus, Denzel. Thus, my fixation on imagination. Because at the bottom of the whole affair, if you can't imagine yourself *into* the text, both imagine its relevance to your life and surrender to where it's taking you, your reading of it will be a sham, done to please a teacher but without bite and effect. Often, we lose them before we even begin.

Creating Open Pedagogical Spaces

I am proposing, therefore, that the challenge for us as teachers is to use the tools of ethnography to investigate literacy narratives, puzzling events, and blank spaces; to respond to the dissonance and the confusion they produce with an attitude of inquiry; to maintain an open pedagogical space so that we can examine our students' understandings and our own. In establishing this open pedagogical space, we allow imagination to enter into our work as teachers and as researchers; we make room in the classroom for doubt, intuition, curiosity, wonder, risk taking, and experimentation; we challenge ourselves and our students to shift our perspectives on teaching and learning. Such a shift will inevitably conflict with prevailing opinions on the "appropriate" roles for teachers and students in conventional classrooms and in schools, because the ways we view curriculum, standards, and assessment will change. In order to illustrate what happens when imagination begins to reconfigure how we define teaching and how we shape curriculum, I will introduce the work of a group of children I taught in the year following my work with the first graders described in Chapter 3.

REIMAGINING CURRICULUM AND CLASSROOM

When asked about my favorite age to teach, I have always declared that there are actually a few grade levels I most enjoy: kindergarten, first and second grade, and fourth grade. When I taught fourth graders in a Gifted and Talented program, they seemed to me still childlike and enthusiastic about school, full of opinions and creativity, but generally with the advantage of being on their way to fluency in reading and writing. The fourth graders I had taught were risk takers and explorers, and very socially conscious, always wanting to understand and remedy social problems. Thus, when I was asked to teach fourth grade for the first time in a regular classroom, I was delighted, although I knew the change in students' ability level would create a big challenge.

In fact, the fourth graders who joined me that year did confirm my love for the age. They were bright, experimental, and tirelessly enthusiastic about learning, providing the same kinds of surprises that I had always experienced with early childhood learners. Six years later as I was working on this book, I found myself returning to the data from that fourth-grade year.

Because I was teaching a new grade level, I had not set out to broaden my exploration of imagination, but I had collected a lot of data. When I reviewed the data from that year, however, I began to consider how my research on imagination had influenced the development and process of our studies in fourth grade and whether my teaching had changed as a result of my research on imagination. The data that follow describe the kinds of decisions I made as I worked collaboratively with my students and how those decisions did, in fact, represent changes in my approach to my teaching and the development of curriculum.

Creating Spaces for Imagination

That August, when I stepped into a classroom full of desks and not much else, I considered how to create a learning space that signaled my interest in the development of my students' creative and imaginative life. In the primary grades, classroom spaces for young children are meant to be rich in materials and design—spaces that encourage language, creativity, and social interaction. I very much wanted to create an interesting physical space for my fourth graders that would encourage the same kinds of learning my first graders had experienced, a space that would also satisfy my own needs for a stimulating and flexible classroom environment.

When my 22 students arrived, though, they were shocked. Where, they asked, were the desks and the rows? Where would they keep their stuff? I explained my philosophy about classroom environments and showed them the storage spaces each would have, the locations of work folders and books. I took them on an explanatory tour of the classroom and explained why I had created math, art, science, writing, and construction areas. I explained that as they were introduced to new materials, those materials would then become available to them to use in the early morning work period, in their work in different subjects, and when they had free time. They were skeptical. Kristie's opinion was representative of the class's opinion of my space: "This classroom," Kristie said bluntly, "doesn't look like a classroom to me."

Being fourth graders, however, meant that they were daring, courageous, and still benevolent enough to want to humor their new teacher. They agreed to try it out, dutifully storing their backpacks outside the classroom, and their notebooks, pencils, and school supplies in cubbies. We established a daily schedule that allowed for quiet artwork in the early morning; a block of morning work time that integrated social studies or science with reading, writing, art, and performance; a late-morning class meeting in which we shared stories and jokes and discussed class governance; a whole-class read-aloud time after lunch, followed by a block of work time that focused on math; and a quiet choice time at the end of the day, when students continued project work or worked with other kinds of classroom materials and manipulatives. At the end of the day we met to revisit what we'd done and share our work. After 2 weeks, when asked, they admitted that they had adjusted to the strange classroom environment and were even proud of it. They started to bring friends from other classes, siblings, and parents to visit after school, giving them explanatory tours, introducing them to our pet cockatiels who sat on their shoulders as they worked, explaining the plantings in the Grow Lab, and showing the art materials we used for projects.

Life was good. But I do have to admit that I was also trying to figure out how to balance my desire for a creative developmental classroom with the increased emphasis that fourth grade places on content, outcomes, and organizational skills. My students naturally adapted to my teaching style and goals. They were still childlike and interested in play and personal expression, but I also saw that a disorganized, free-floating fourth grader (and there were many of them, mostly boys) was very different from a disorganized, free-floating first grader. I had a responsibility to help those students begin to comprehend how to systematically work on content, outcomes, and organization, even as I was committed to developing a rich learning environment and an imaginative, expressive curriculum.

What I found over the course of the year was that the two areas were not, in fact, opposed to one another. Rather, all the creative work we did as part of our content-area studies both required and motivated my students to be more organized, goal oriented, and involved with content. Often they, not I, asked for more responsibility for developing the outcomes of our work, and they, not I, emphasized in our class meetings that if people didn't have their facts right, or weren't taking responsibility for carrying their weight in a group project, they weren't going to produce a good piece of work. However, their desire to become a community and exercise self-determination over their affairs was not without difficulties. Many class meetings were contentious as they worked out guidelines for good small-group work and classroom procedures, but they never lost their enthusiasm for the journey.

Framing the Social Studies Curriculum: A Focus on Survival

After spending the summer acquainting myself with the school district's curriculum for each subject in fourth grade, I began the year with a plan to use the social studies curriculum as a focal point for our work throughout the year. That curriculum consisted of a survey of American history from the settling of the Americas to the beginning of westward expansion. Although that period included a daunting amount of political and social history, I felt it offered many opportunities for rich involvement with literature, drama, writing, the arts, math, and even science. I wanted, though, to avoid the entrapment of history in its chronology. In other words, I wanted history to be more than a progression of events over time: to be about daily life, about the impact of historical events in the lives of the people who lived them, and about the relevance of those events to our lives in the present.

As I reviewed the textbooks and materials for the social studies curriculum, I thought about what might be a focusing concept for this period of discovery, settlement, and development that would pull my students into the subject. Personally, I was struck over and over again that at every point the struggle to survive presented itself as a major theme. I concluded that I wanted to frame our studies from the perspective of survival, a concept most of my students would not have had experience with in their lives, but one that had captured my imagination and that I was sure would capture theirs.

Over the course of the year we studied the arrival in America of aboriginal peoples, the cultures of Native Americans and the nature of their encounters with Europeans, the incursions of explorers from Europe, the establishment of the colonies, the events leading up to and through the Revolutionary War, and the beginning of the movement west. From the beginning, when I introduced the idea of survival as a main idea, the children embraced it heartily. They did have a modest working definition of survival ("staying alive"), but their examples came primarily from movies and fiction. They were excited, though, by the possibilities of imagining themselves as survivors through, first, our shared readings of literature, and, later, through work in which we painted, drew, wrote poetry, and dramatized the events of history *not as observers, but as participants*. For example, the data that follow illustrate the kind of involvement with the concept that began to occur early in the year, both in and outside the classroom.

> We've been reading *Maroo of the Winter Caves* [Nicol, 1990] for 2 weeks as our read-aloud to move us into an imaginative place while we consider how people might first have come to this continent and the kinds of difficulties they would have encountered on a daily basis. They are riveted to the book. We've collected vocabulary as we go: *crevice, flay, gore, amulet, carcass, carrion, sinew, ruthless, domesticate.* We've brainstormed what kind of science prehistoric peoples in the Ice Age needed to know to survive. We've made and worn amulets to copy Maroo and her family.
>
> I saw today at recess that Sati and Bobbi have been digging in the dirt for two days now. [This is not something I expect fourth graders to do.] They've got a pile of dirt surrounded by sticks and topped with grass. "We're making a pie. The sticks are the fire around it. We're practicing survival." This afternoon, the children are sketching one of the events in the book, in pairs or alone. It is very quiet. Several children are humming. (Fieldnotes, October 18)

I have to admit that I was loving this work, not only because the children were so engaged but also because of the richness of the content and the wonder it evoked for all of us. Imagining endless snow and ice, the practice of following game wherever it led, killing and butchering that game, preserving the meat, making tools, finding shelter, combating cold and illness—all of these elements provoked intense speculative discussions and artwork.

As the months passed, we moved through studies of exploration and discovery, the arrival of the Puritans and the settling of the East Coast, life in pre-Revolutionary America, and the beginning of the westward settlements in Indian country. Every phase of our studies was centered around historical fiction, some of which we read as a class and some of which we read in reading response groups. Sometimes, for homework assignments, I asked the children to consider an issue of survival. For example, in December, after a whole-class reading of *Hatchet* (Paulsen, 2000), a book that describes the stranding of a boy in a remote area, I asked the class to write a short essay in response to the following questions: "What does survival in our time mean? Were Ice Age peoples better at it than we?"

As we moved back and forth between nonfiction and historical fiction, the children dramatized, wrote, and made murals and posters of historical characters and events. During a reading of *Johnny Tremain* (Forbes, 1943), they were outraged at the living conditions he endured as an indentured servant ("In Boston, of all places!" exclaimed one student) and spent a great deal of time discussing what they would have done to escape his predicament. They were saddened by the accounts describing the capture, killing, and kidnapping of families by settlers and Indians alike, and they energetically discussed whether they would have returned to their families if they had been stolen by Indians.

The Final Project: A Simulation

The final project on survival began in April as an exercise in thinking further about exploration, colonies, and the meaning of colonization. I had brought *The Green Book* (Paton, 1982) to class because I wanted them to synthesize the knowledge they had been gathering over the course of the year. I was also responding to their strong interest in science fiction and space exploration. In *The Green Book,* the author shifts the notion of colonization to a futuristic setting that my students found extremely compelling. As the book opens, the people of earth have used up all of their resources and the planet can no longer support human life. A small group of people living in England are offered the opportunity to leave in search of a habitable planet. The story chronicles, first, the kinds of decisions they must make about what to bring with them and what to leave, and, later, their efforts to learn about the new environment they settle in and how to establish a viable colony.

The book grabbed the class's attention not only because it mirrored so closely the problems we had discussed all year in the context of survival but also because the class had been very involved throughout the year in discussions about the future of the earth and the peoples that inhabit it. For example, in early October they asked the following questions in their Science Talks (Gallas, 1995):

Why do people say the earth will end?
Why doesn't the earth crash into the stars?
Is the world alive?
How did people learn to survive?
How long could we survive without the sun?

We read the book and the children begged for another—"a sequel or even a prequel!" Lacking either of those, we hatched the idea of doing our own sequel by creating a simulation around the premise of the book: We would become the explorers, abandoning our planet to travel and settle another unknown world of our own creation.

COLONIZING A NEW PLANET

The work that came out of this project was both substantive and imaginative. It was substantive because, as the reader will see, many of the themes and concepts we had studied throughout the year were reframed and extended in the process of the ongoing performance of the simulation. It was imaginative in that we had no guidelines when we started the simulation except those that were part of the structure of Paton's book: We were traveling with one precious belonging; we were searching for a habitable planet; we could take only those things deemed absolutely essential for our basic survival; when we arrived, our job would be to explore and colonize the new planet. Nothing else was determined. The content of the simulation and our actions within it came from our collective imagination.

Defining the Characters

Each class member was allowed to choose who they were and what their role would be, and we all worked on the simulation *in character* 2 afternoons a week for 2 months. During the work periods, maps of the planet and planetoid were produced; flora and fauna were identified, sketched, and labeled; shelters and tools were designed; music was composed; plants and animals were collected and tested as food sources; illnesses were identified, diagnosed, and treated; governance structures were invented; expeditions to explore the different regions of the planet were launched; and an ongoing narrative was written recording the activities of the group. After each working session, we had what we called a "Report Out," in which community members updated the group on what they had been doing.

The group decided that I had to be "the Guide." I had asked to be able to choose another role, but they insisted they needed a Guide, just as Paton had in her book, and they said I was "the logical person, since, actually, you really are our guide because you're our teacher." Here are the roles they've chosen:

Astrophysicist: Lucas, who says he has already begun an exploration of the planet from space and has discovered that our planet is a tetrahedron. He explains the details of our sun, the constellations, our orbit, etc.

Physicians: Sati, Louis, and Bobbi. Sati says she is a pathologist. Bobbi is a pediatrician. Sati and Bobbi are keeping notes in their journals. Louis, who is a surgeon, is keeping his notes on an Alpha Smart Pro [a laptop keyboard]. Each describes their discoveries about the disease organisms of the planet to the group.

Housing organizers: Alex, Brad, Matthew.

Designers: Mona, Boris, Michaela, who are designing furniture, tools, machines for us, also taking requests for needed objects.

Laws: Sasha, Kristie, Joshua, who are working on a draft of the laws and governance structure, including a Bill of Rights.

Food experts: Lizzie and Ana, who are testing plants and animals for edibility and making up new recipes using available ingredients.

Historians: Loti and Jane, both keeping journals.

Composer: Brenden, who is working on our first piece of music. [See Figure 8.2.] He spends a great deal of time debating what key to compose in. During our new planet work time, I have observed him sitting and singing to himself, transcribing the melody, absolutely in character.

Explorers: Jin and Kei, who are preparing an expedition to the far side of the planet, during which they will map the terrain and collect and sketch flora and fauna. [See Figure 8.3.]

FIGURE 8.2. Brenden's composition

"The finder": Thomas. We'll see what that means. I think it might be some kind of natural scientist. Thomas says he will help Jin and Kei with their work. (Report Out, April 28)

While working in character, the students began to produce an unprecedented amount of writing, maps, and artwork. Each character produced documents that were appropriate to his or her role. For example, Figures 8.2 and 8.3 were presented and explained as part of the Report Out on April 28. Figure 8.2, done by our composer, shows a piece of sheet music he was working on. Figure 8.3 was one of several scientific drawings done of the plant life found growing on our planet. Below is an example of physician's notes written by "Dr. Bobbi" in a bound journal she was keeping.

Peggy Seward, age 17: Broke her leg while hiking. I brought plaster with me (a cast) and I'll make crutches out of wood and make the cushion that goes under her clavicle, and phalanges out of feather, and wrap the cloth around the feathers and it might mend.

Karen Judge, age 15: Two boys knocked her down and she sprained her tarsals. I'll do the same thing I did to Seward.

Nancy Simon, age 11: Ate Yellow Petal Flower without grinding and her large intestines are a pale sky blue. I'll have to talk to Dr. Louis, the surgeon, to see if Nancy needs an intestine-ectomy. (Notes from Dr. Bobbi's journal)

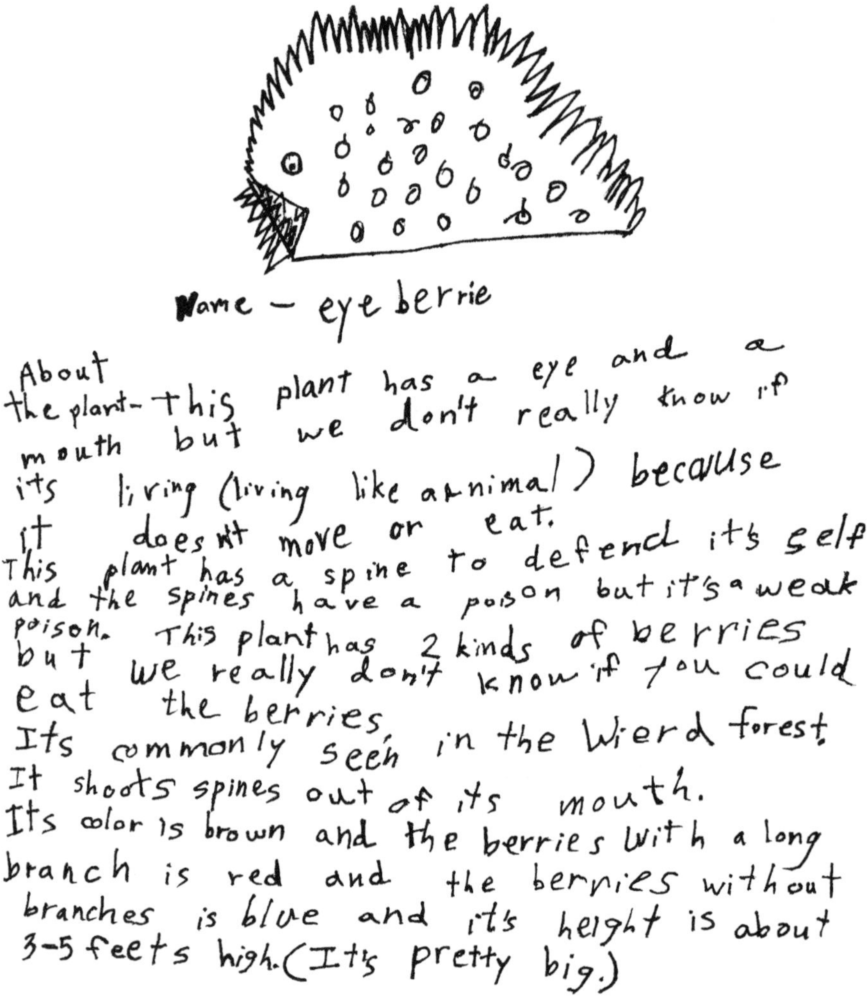

Name — eye berrie

About the plant- This plant has a eye and a mouth but we don't really know if its living (living like an nimal) because it doesn't move or eat. This plant has a spine to defend it's self and the spines have a poison but it's a weak poison. This plant has 2 kinds of berries but we really don't know if you could eat the berries. Its commonly seen in the Wierd forest. It shoots spines out of its mouth. Its color is brown and the berries With a long branch is red and the berries without branches is blue and it's height is about 3-5 feets high. (It's pretty big.)

FIGURE 8.3. "Eyeberries"

Note, here, how Bobbi incorporated her developing anatomical knowledge and vocabulary, stemming from her real-life interest in being a doctor, and information from the research of her fellow scientists on the planet. As her teacher, I noted the different tone in this piece of writing: In her physician's notes "Dr. Bobbi" was confident and authoritative, in contrast to Bobbi, the student, who was shy, hesitant, and took no risks.

Governance of the New World

The class became very engaged with issues surrounding the governance of their new colony. This work was a direct extension of our studies earlier in the year of the structure of our democratic institutions—a mandated part of the fourth-grade social studies curriculum. Their discussions were also colored by their vigorous engagement with the presidential election the previous fall. The legal team drew a distinction between the colony's Bill of Rights and the laws that would make life in a hostile environment orderly. They outlined the laws in more depth at the Report Outs and asked for the group's approval. The laws included the following:

> When making an important decision, majority rules.
> No hoarding life-sustaining supplies.
> No one is above the law. ("Which basically means that nobody can not follow the rules, because they're too important.")
> No physically or mentally hurting any living things, unless you need to for food or something.
> No one may do anything unplanned without permission from the Guide.
> Do not take any unnecessary risks.
> No hunting, unless it's in season.
> You must pay the taxes.

Taxes. The subject of taxes, more than any other issue, elicited, as it does with adults, a vigorous discussion of what their purpose would be in a newly established and relatively impoverished community. It seemed to me as I listened that the legal team of Sasha, Joshua, and Kristie had thoroughly considered the idea of taxes among themselves and were ready for objections. Moreover, in looking at the questions and kinds of exchanges that ensued, it was interesting to see that their roles as players in the simulation figured heavily in the ways they shaped their arguments. In the following discussion, the reader will see the energetic and sometimes contentious discourse that developed around the topic of governance.

> **GUIDE:** Can we hear [??] please, because this becomes an anarchistic discussion. You all recall what that word means? If you have something to say . . . But first, I'd like this group to explain what taxes are for and what they do.

SASHA: They, like, help the housing people build the houses.
KRISTIE: Right.

[simultaneous conversations]

JOSHUA: So the government can do things for the people. It's like . . .
The reason you pay taxes here is so that they can help the people
in the country.

[simultaneous conversations]

BRAD: But what's the point of having taxes now? I mean, we're working
as a group to at least live, so why would we need taxes right now?
I mean, maybe in the future we could use taxes, but not right now.
MICHAELA: We don't even really have money right now.
MATTHEW: We haven't even started to build our houses yet, so why
would we need taxes?

[simultaneous conversations]

KRISTIE: We weren't thinking of money; we're thinking of barter.
SASHA: Trading.
JOSHUA: A string of corn, like one piece of corn or something like
that, that's barter, trading and stuff. So that we can make the
country better.
LUCAS: But what is the point? Because, I mean, we don't have to pay
for the houses, since we're kind of a group; and as far as we know
we're the only people on the planet, or, like, intelligent life.
JIN: Except for the Rollerbob. [See Figure 8.4.] (Report Out, May 3)

Electoral System. Kristie, Joshua, and Sasha were bullish in their role
as legislative advisers, insisting that the class consider every aspect of governance and come to consensus about the structures they were putting in
place. In this final phase of their work, they presented what they called "the
presidential laws," and the class considered how to elect their representa-
tives and what to do if they disagreed with their elected officials.

KRISTIE: The president must keep the laws enforced. If the president
and Congress disagree, the people decide.
JOSHUA: The people can't act, like, unruly.
GUIDE: No, but they'll be able to decide.
KRISTIE: Everyone must vote and make two nominations. You have
to make two nominations for a boy and a girl. If everyone truly

Height: 2'   Width: 10"
Inedible!
Color: Purple with a green jumper.
Habitat: Everywhere
Can sleep whenever!
Common!!
Extremly smart, extremely
Cute, Can glide for
Short periods.
Arch Enemy is the devil bird.
Extremely friendly.
Speaks 10 million languages.

We talked to one and He
said "We want to help you
adapt to our planet. But you
will help us fight the Devil
Birds."
Eats the fun-gus and the
Bob-leaf

FIGURE 8.4. "The Rollerbob"

dislikes the president's decisions and actions, they can impeach
him or her.

ALEX: Like Richard Nixon. Like [??]

KRISTIE: We're going to elect a president every 3 weeks.

LUCAS: Every 3 weeks?

KRISTIE: We don't have much time left in school.

GUIDE: We'll pretend it's years.

SASHA: Yeah. Every 3 years.

The Process of the Simulation

As the weeks passed, the daily simulation became more routinized. Everyone would immediately go to work when the time for the simulation arrived, picking up on the work from a few days earlier as if time had not passed in between sessions. As they worked, small dramas began to take place. The dramas were often brought to the whole group in the Report Outs, and they would develop further as the group discussed them. The following notes from a Report Out give the flavor of their daily work and offer a glimpse of the priceless dramatic moments that often resulted from the group's deliberations.

> We vote on the name of the planet. Planet Vengar wins. Loti and Jane say they will write an anthem.
>
> Thomas reports that the soil is hard and the rocks can be very light. They might be useful for writing tools. The water tastes like grape juice and Dr. Seuss trees do have sap.
>
> Jin and Kei share their map of the planet and show us the route they took in their explorations.
>
> Sasha and Kristie are building a voting booth for the presidential elections.
>
> The doctors report to the group that they have been dismayed to discover that Susan brought her cats with her on the space ship, deliberately breaking the group's agreed-upon rule that no pets could be brought to the new planet. Brad says, "We'll have to kill the cats." Susan cries! (No way, no kidding! She's really crying! This is not pretend.) She gets up to blow her nose, and as she does, Lucas declares he also brought earthworms with him. I say that the legislators will have to decide what should be done. Susan calms herself a bit.
>
> Sati describes three new diseases and the remedies the doctors have discovered. Louis describes a virus one person caught from an amphibian they are still trying to identify.
>
> The housing people report they have completed an office and are working on a jail. Brad says, looking pointedly at Susan, "in case we need one." (Report Out, May 5)

The incident with Susan over the cats astounded me. I had clearly underestimated the earnestness with which some students were playing their roles.

There were also growing signs that the simulation was beginning to have a liberating effect on other students. I have already referred to "Dr. Bobbi," whose work in the simulation was qualitatively more ambitious and influential than her work prior to the simulation. Lucas, who was very gifted, was another student who was quite transformed when he worked in character. Uncomfortable with and unused to interacting socially with his peers, Lucas began fourth grade on the fringes of the class, finding it difficult to concentrate on his work and participate in his classmates' exchanges and games. Over the course of the year, he did become more comfortable socially, but the simulation had a dramatic effect on his work habits and his presentation of self. Whenever he had extra time during the day, Lucas worked on the drawings of the explorations he was doing for the simulation. He paid extraordinarily close attention to every detail of the Report Outs: eyes on the speaker, making contributions to the discussions, never distracted. (Actually, everyone was quite attentive. I didn't have to police group behavior at all.) Lucas was also actively interacting with all the students in the class as part of his role: requesting designers to work on things for him and builders to construct a space station, offering to help the physicians because he had "a background in biology as well as in astrophysics" (and that was true).

As normally reticent students like Susan, Bobbi, and Lucas became more invested in their roles, they began to influence the direction of the simulation itself. The following notes were written by Loti, the planet historian.

> Susan didn't give her two cats to the laboratory. Both cats are sick. Punishment: Take her cats to the East. (Susan can come.) If the Devil Birds get sick, it means her two cats have to be put to sleep. We're worried about it. Something else could happen. Could her cats die? We don't know about death on this planet.
>
> The Devil Bird may have a use. We need a spy researcher like Jane Goodall. Maybe Susan, as a punishment.
>
> Lucas's worms are doing well. Softening up the soil. (Notes from Loti's journal)

During a Report Out, the saga of unlawful pets continued.

> Alex admits to the group that he has a dog with him—"a corgi," he says with a smile. The group is outraged, but Alex is calm. Susan manages a little smile in his direction.

The legislators (Kristie, Sasha, Joshua) call for nominations for president. The group nominates Brad, Mona, Louis, and Jane. Jane wins the election. The legislators then turn their attention to the cat problem and ask Jane to make a judgment. They confer and then announce that they've decided that the cats will be put in the physicians' care. Susan can visit the cats, but she can't take them away. She must also use her own food supply to feed them. Jane says, "If the cat becomes seriously ill and endangers us, we kill it." Susan cries again, especially when Jane tells her the cat will be killed if it endangers the planet. Susan asks me for permission to speak to Jane directly. She says, as tears run down her cheeks, "Jane, I'd appreciate it if you could say *put to sleep* instead of *killed.*" Jane graciously says, "that would be fine." (Report Out, May 7)

Adaptation and Disease

Finally, late in May, the simulation took a new turn. The doctors, led by Dr. Bobbi, took a leadership role and began to identify helpful organisms as well as different kinds of diseases and biological threats. The following summary, as reported by Loti in her weekly issue of "Planet Vengar News," shows the changing direction of the group's work.

Dr. Sati found a new kind of bacteria. The doctor says trees can be used for bedding and are edible, and cure Gellato, and are useful for building houses. Lucas says that the planet is triangular. And there's a beer can shape orbiting the planet, maybe a planetoid. We are getting many new things like a solar powered TV, an oven for the chefs, a new closet, and a berry picker.

We are having trouble with the lack of bathrooms.

Watch out for Frecklejuice, Gellato, and Okleoupious. Okleoupious is a cold. Frecklejuice is a mental disease. Gellato is a disease when you get a green square on your back and you get a black face and it causes lots of pain. So please tell our doctors if you or a friend might have a sickness.

On May 29, Dr. Bobbi came to me for a private conversation. She reported that she was treating Mona and Bonnie for a mysterious ailment. She said to me, "They seem to have gone back in time. They're acting like children."

In fact, when I looked across the room, Bonnie was sitting in a chair, spinning it and saying, "Dizzy duck, dizzy duck," over and over. Mona was under a chair saying, "Cook fish, cook fish." In the Report Out that followed, Bobbi reported on Bonnie and Mona. Her voice was loud and clear, and she had written a report and collected pictures from others in the group showing the symptoms. Louis, also a physician, reported that Matthew was having similar symptoms. As we listened to his report, several children in the group began to shake and show strange symptoms. Later in the afternoon, the doctors were working in a corner of the classroom with the "ailing" students. They were staying completely in character. In fact, everyone in the room was in character. Not surprisingly, the "disease" continued to spread during each session of the simulation.

> In this session the doctors have confirmed that something is biting the members of the community. About half the children begin the session as babbling idiots. (I surmise that the fun of acting like a baby has surfaced in this imaginative exercise because it has real appeal for fourth graders who are being pressed on all sides to act more grownup.) As the Guide, I see a danger for our planet (and for our simulation).
> I have started to intervene, going to each physician privately and telling them how worried I am about the illness—that it's depleting our work force and jeopardizing our survival. Then I requested that the patients be sedated so the physicians can work on remedies. The physicians reluctantly subdued their patients who (reluctantly) went to sleep. Within 30 seconds, the first group had a miraculous cure, and they rushed back to work with their healthy compatriots. The second group, with Bobbi, which is the original group to fall ill last session during their trip to the planetoid, were harder. They were delirious and babbling. Bobbi was rushing between them, trying to comfort and administer to them. I pulled her aside and gave her the same sedation spiel. She reluctantly sedated them, and they fell into a restless sleep. (Fieldnotes, June 9)

Following the sedation of the patients, the physicians and I conferred. Bobbi authoritatively reviewed the onset of symptoms she had recorded in her journal and the progression of the disease, and she shared her notes and drawings. Louis responded that her information was similar to his. At that point, I left them to check on other groups in the classroom. Then Kristie, Sasha, and Thomas fell ill. Immediately I saw we were about to have a crisis (of order!), since half the class was delirious with fever. I called a meeting and stated my fears to those members of the colony who were still healthy. The rest of the invalids were sleeping fitfully, although somehow they had managed to join the circle with those of us who were discussing the problem. There was a serious discussion about alternatives for us in the face of the new crisis:

1. Stay and build protective fences from the animals that are infecting us.
2. Move to the planetoid. "But," says one student, "that's where they first got sick!"
3. Set up remote sensors to search for better living areas, to see the animal activity on the planet or planetoid, and to watch the patients so that the doctors can get some rest.
4. Go back to earth or another location.

Suddenly, Loti said she felt better. She mused that she might have been cured by the pillow she'd been resting on. She passed the pillow to Sasha, who soon felt better as well. Soon, everyone was cured and the doctors resolved to study the pillow.

The next day, as we came in from lunch, Joshua said he thought maybe we should train some psychiatrists for the new planet. I asked why.

JOSHUA: Well, maybe some of the sickness isn't really in their bodies.
KAREN: You mean it's in their heads?
JOSHUA: Yeah.
KAREN: So it's psychosomatic?
JOSHUA: *(looks puzzled)*
KAREN: Oh, I mean it's in their heads, but they feel sick in their bodies, so they think they're really sick.
JOSHUA: Yeah.

That exchange was one of many that were taking place outside of the simulation time regarding the events of the simulation itself. For the most part, those conversations did not occur in more traditional instructional times—the children were careful not to bring the simulation into other parts of the day (a rule we had established early on)—but they did signal that the problems raised in the simulation were being worked on at other times in the day.

By the second week in June, our situation had not improved. My field-notes record the events that led to the final resolution of the problem.

> We are processing what to do. Many are still sick or falling sick. After the meeting, we move into our work session, and more fall sick. I quarantine them, and Bobbi dispenses antidotes (jellybears she has brought from home) to each sick worker. Still, the sick don't get better. Finally, as I peruse the situation, I make a unilateral decision. I walk into the "sick room" and inform the patients that if they don't get better, I will have no choice but to kill them.
>
> "Why?" they ask, looking shocked.
>
> I respond, "Because you are using up precious resources: food, water, medication; and you're not improving. You're endangering us all."
>
> "Ewww," they answer as a group.
>
> A minute later they are cured. (Fieldnotes, June 9)

RECLAIMING, RENAMING, REIMAGINING THE CLASSROOM

When I revisited these fieldnotes more than 2 years later, I was shocked at the way in which the problem of the simulation was resolved. Never, in my wildest dreams of any teaching moment that might have occurred in the 30 or more years I have taught, would I have believed that I might walk into a group of children engaged in classwork and tell them I was going to have to kill them. Of course, I now realize that never in my history as a teacher had I so completely joined in a classroom activity, both as teacher and as co-actor. At the moment I reread that excerpt, I laughed out loud at the outrageousness of my statement and at my memories of the astonished looks on the faces of my students as well as my own surprise when those words came out of my mouth. They were speechless, but I, as the Guide, was dead serious. Our life on Vengar was endangered by their actions. I had no idea, however, how they would react. After all, we were all players in a simulation that had never been carried out before. On a small level, we were playing out the game of survival without knowing the outcome, just as all the explorers throughout history have pursued their goals without any knowledge of the final outcome.

Valuing Imagination, Collaboration, and Improvisation

How do I see the value of this exercise in developing a curriculum with imagination as the centerpiece? What potential does such an approach have for reshaping how we approach our role as teachers? The simulation, when viewed as an imaginative collaborative exercise, offered many opportunities for deep learning, synthesis of knowledge, and social growth. If I break out what we were learning in relation to the goals of our social studies curriculum, it was huge: understanding the concept of survival as more than providing for basic needs of food and shelter, designing a governance system, mapping the regions of the planet, and identifying the interpersonal issues of surviving as a colonizing community. Yet the simulation also clearly grabbed the attention and energy of certain children in ways they had not shown all year. For example, Lucas, Susan, and Bobbi, who had never been confident in the class, were completely engaged. All of them began to join in the Report Outs, speaking loudly and clearly while in character, interacting with other children when before they had been isolated, clearly influencing the development of the simulation itself. The simulation used the children's imaginative capacities to make an idea (colonization, survival) real, and it also changed our social relationships.

In this process, the importance of the literature we had previously read together cannot be overestimated: *Sylvester and the Magic Pebble* (Steig, 1987), *Brave Irene* (Steig, 1986b), *Abel's Island* (Steig, 1986a), *Maroo of the Winter Caves* (Nicol, 1990), *Wind in the Willows* (Graham, 1980), *Hatchet* (Paulsen, 2000), *Johnny Tremain* (Forbes, 1943), *Indian Captive: The Story of Mary Jemison* (Lenski, 1995), *Sign of the Beaver* (Speare, 1988), *Freedom Train* (Sterling, 1954), *The Courage of Sarah Noble* (Dalgliesh, 1991), *Sing Down the Moon* (O'Dell, 1970), *Grasshopper Summer* (Turner, 1989), *Wagon Wheels* (Brenner & Bolognese, 1993), and *Save Queen of Sheba* (Moeri, 1981). These rich works of literature enabled us to be involved with the dramas of history through our imaginations. During the simulation, I saw that the characters the children took on were extensions of the survival characters we had met in those books. And finally, after rereading the transcripts of the Report Outs, most especially the discussions on the governance structure, it was clear how, when engaged as performers within the context of creating an imaginary society, the children worked with ideas of law, economics, and democracy by pulling together many of the discussions and readings we had done in the course of studying the foundations of the early American republic.

Collaborating as Imaginators

My original goal for the simulation had been to move history beyond its chronology into the realm of imagination and identification. That certainly seemed to have happened. But on consideration, I believe that movement occurred as a result of our *collaboration as imaginators*. Had I taken a more traditional stance and stood on the sidelines observing and directing, the outcome would, in my opinion, have been quite different. Straight through the project I was working in the role the students had asked me to take. I was the Guide who helped them make decisions in times of crisis; I actively worked with each group, and/or individuals, to find out what they were working on; and I encouraged them to find their own direction in the roles they had chosen. All of those aspects of my role might seem at first to be nothing more than myself acting as myself, the teacher. But the distinction between myself as Guide on Planet Vengar and myself as teacher in a fourth-grade classroom can be found in the fact that during the simulation, I, like my students, acted only in the imaginary context of Planet Vengar and our quest as colonizers. I did not direct the action in order to determine what was done and how it was done. I did not direct the students to work on governance, disease, history, geography, science, art, invention, literature, or music. Those pursuits, and others, emerged naturally through our active engagement with imagination and the knowledge we had gained throughout the year.

Yet my capacity to take on that role of co-actor also emanated from my own process of conducting an ethnography of imagination. From my first encounter with Denzel, I had sought to understand how imagination worked, both through documenting my observations and interactions with children and through exploring my own process of imagination and what others had written about it. It was inevitable that my involvement in the ethnography gradually changed how I carried out my role as a teacher, reshaping my interactions with my students and my approach to curriculum, blurring the boundaries that separated me, as teacher and adult, from my students, as children and learners, enabling my students and myself to reclaim, rename, and reimagine our classroom. In the end, I think, believing in the importance of imagination and living actively with it from day to day can have no other result.

CHAPTER 9

"Entering the Rabbit Hole"

Science has been impressively successful, but every accumulation of knowledge, like the earthen bank on which I sit, is full of rabbit holes. Enter a rabbit hole—into quantum physics, say, or relativity and that Wonderland has its own rabbit holes leading to yet other exotic terrains. One doesn't have to be a Lord Kelvin or a Planck or an Einstein to find a rabbit hole to enter. A pebble can serve—if I choose to enter it. A leaf of grass will provide ingress to infinity. (Raymo, 1987, p. 174)

In *Honey from Stone* (1987), Raymo describes, from his vantage point as a naturalist, how, when imagination is closely tied to observation, deduction, logic, even detailed calculations of phenomena in the natural world, it naturally raises questions and conclusions that fly in the face of what is believed to be true. He cites the work of Aristarchus, who proposed around 200 B.C. that the diameter of the sun was seven times that of the earth. From that incorrect but audacious and heretical theory, Aristarchus concluded correctly that the earth orbited the sun and, further, his observations of the stars suggested that they were fixed in space and that therefore the size of the universe must be infinitely large. Raymo (1987) writes:

The heresy of Aristarchus was the heresy of scale, like the heresy of Job and the heresy of Galileo. Aristarchus dared to suggest that the creation was not measured on a human scale. And yet, in his works the human imagination is stretched to encompass an infinite creation. The bold theorems of Aristarchus are prayers that address the infinity of the world; his mathematical propositions are the language of praise. (p. 40)

Through Aristarchus, Raymo suggests that the active pursuit of wonder and imaginative thinking is logically followed by the reconstruction and rearrangement of knowledge, and that each achievement or mastery of an idea only opens up more "rabbit holes" to be pursued and more mystery

164

to be perceived. As Raymo says, "Description is revelation. Seeing is praise" (p. 185). To me, this raises the idea that education must create a new paradigm about the cycle of learning and what its goals might be. As I said in Chapter 8, educators must reclaim, rename, and reimagine teaching and learning. Raymo proposes that the goal be one of "praise" for the complexity of the world and openness to questions that have not been asked and seem unanswerable. What kind of educational outcome is this? Do we call this just "excitement about learning," or is it more: the cultivation of wonder through observation and questioning, openness to not knowing, valuing the unanswerable?

A NEW PARADIGM

We are having a class recital to celebrate different kinds of "talent." This is in response to Nat's request to play a selection from his piano recital. This is a record of who did what.

1. Nat plays "Deck the Halls."
2. Ellie has a magic trick using a tall cowboy hat. She has the hat on. It covers her eyes. She turns away and pulls a little rabbit out from under the crown of the hat.
3. Betty does rubberband tricks while she tells jokes.
4. Katie plays "Jingle Bells" with chords on a toy piano.
5. Tommy plays maracas. We have to guess what he is. "A crazy monkey!"
6. Brian does a magic trick.
7. Jamilla mimes a leopard.
8. Sophia has two eggs that are shakers. She asks for a helper, chooses Barbara. They throw the eggs back and forth.
9. Jamilla says she has another. She chooses Ellie as a partner. She lays out some markers, gives Ellie some, picks the rest up, and throws one at her. Ellie does the same. They continue to fling markers at one another one at a time. (By this time, Sarah and I are laughing hysterically; we are close to delirious.)
10. Sasha sings, or starts to sing, "Somewhere over the Rainbow." She gets shy, says she's been practicing and can say the words. So she recites the words. Then Jamilla stands up and walks up to her, saying she'll sing it. And she does, in a beautiful voice. I look around

> the group of children and see several children mouthing the
> words. Emily is swaying back and forth, as if in a trance. Katie is
> staring off into the distance, mouthing the lyrics. (Fieldnotes,
> December 21)

Here we have a description of children and teachers engaged in a community event. We were, as Lessing (1994) describes it, in a "Wordsworthian
'spot of time' . . . open to experience and also aware of heightened openness, aware that the moment is privileged" (p. 54). What we were experi-
encing there was play, art, and imagination moving us. But toward what?
Joy, as C. S. Lewis (1956) proposes? Artistic transformation? Or, and I say
this fearfully, the soaring of the imagination toward the divine?

JOY?

Dare I say, as a teacher in a secular system, that a goal of education should
be the realization of joy, the divine, or the mysterious—that we should cul-
tivate, in our teaching, encounters with the sublime? The idea smacks of public school heresy and religious fervor, but it is an idea that my reading and
research for this project have continuously returned to. Nabokov (1967), for
example, in describing his work as a lepidopterist, notes how love, ecstasy,
and metaphysical awareness were part of his work as a scientist:

> The highest enjoyment of timelessness is when I stand among rare butter-
> flies and their food plants. This is ecstasy, and behind the ecstasy is some-
> thing else, which is hard to explain. It is like a momentary vacuum into
> which rushes all that I love. A sense of oneness with sun and stone. A thrill
> of gratitude to whom it may concern. (p. 139)

He describes a similar moment when he wrote his first poem in the moments following a thunderstorm:

> A moment later my first poem began. What touched it off? I think I know.
> Without any wind blowing, the sheer weight of a raindrop, shining in par-
> asitic luxury on a cordate leaf, caused its tip to dip, and what looked like a
> globule of quick-silver performed a sudden glissando down the center vein,
> and then, having shed its bright load,the relieved leaf unbent. Tip, leaf, dip,
> relief—the instant it all took to happen seemed to me not so much a frac-

tion of time as a fissure in it, a missed heartbeat, which was refunded at once by a patter of rhymes. . . . The stanza I was muttering resembled the shock of wonder I had experienced when for a moment heart and leaf had been one. (p. 217)

In autobiographical accounts by scientists and artists, philosophers and theologians, when moments of deep insight and learning occur, these moments are described almost exclusively as occurring *out of school*, when a child or an adult was in a state of unselfconscious openness to the world. The mind is open. Imagination moves into the moment and transforms it into a kind of learning that is deep, personal, and intangible. Why must most of those moments occur out of school?

IMAGINATION AND EDUCATION

The imagination is a hidden art in the depths of the soul whose true devices nature will scarcely let us divine and spread exposed before our eyes. (Kant, 1786/1969, p. 181)

But now I've backed myself into my own rabbit hole. As I said in the beginning of this book, the subject of imagination has always been more than I could handle. I take solace in the fact that most people who write about imagination acknowledge that it is also bigger than they. And so, after stating that imagination and learning, when paired, can lead to joy, ecstasy, and encounters with the sublime, and that that is what education ought to be about, I find that I am stuck. I am treading on forbidden ground. All my years in public education have almost rendered me unable to proceed—unable to imagine what schools would look like if imagination were recognized as the necessary center of learning and growth. This is not something I can do alone, as my students have taught me. Imagining new educational worlds is a project that would require us to throw aside so many assumptions about the world and the purposes of education. For that, you need the collaboration of other imaginators who are committed to joy, transformation, and the development of broader understandings of what constitutes learning.

That, most probably, is why imagination is the unspoken power of mind that schools do not attend to, except when we sometimes allow it to surface in more marginalized subjects, such as art and music. Because when imagination is allowed to rise up and do the work of transformation, the work and the transformation that occur in both students and teachers cannot be quantified into "acceptable" forms. That is, the outcomes of such learning won't fit within the framework of "measurable outcomes," standardized tests, rubrics, programmed learning. The process of such learning won't fit into stipulated time slots or scripted texts for subject-matter instruction. The social alterations of such learning shift power and authority from the teacher alone to teacher and students, and that, above all, will provoke discomfort in those who most fear disorder, those who believe that disorder (talk, movement, laughter, joy?) is not present in serious learning environments, those who believe that disorder means loss of control and that loss of control is always dangerous.

RECLAIMING IMAGINATION

To reimagine education and overcome our fear of what we cannot control, we must turn our attention back to the children and remind ourselves that, evidence to the contrary, our educational system is meant to serve the interests and well-being of children rather than those of adults. For myself, I want to consider, specifically, a child who is not yet born. As the reader may recall, a portion of my research on imagination was done with the assistance of my then-intern, Sarah. Sarah contributed to that work through her fieldnotes and through her openness to the children and myself: Everything we did surprised and delighted her. I have spent the last 6 months looking at our mutually kept journal, scanning her handwritten notes, reading and rereading her questions.

Sarah sent me an e-mail yesterday informing me that she was in labor. Sarah, giving birth to this child, cannot know what her child will become, but she and her husband will imagine a life for their child, and from that imagined life they will shape and reshape their own lives. Part of what they will consider will be their child's education: what kind of school he or she will attend, whether the teachers are caring and respectful, whether their child's persona will be valued and cared for, to what extent their child is accepted and loved by his classmates, and, finally, whether their child's inborn capacities and gifts, which will become partially evident to them in the years before school, can be realized in school. And that, of course, is the crux of the problem.

Our children begin their schooling full with imagination. As George Dennison (1969) writes, "Children are so powerfully attracted to this world that the very motion of their curiosity comes through to us as a form of love" (p. 9). They are open to joy, curiosity, wonder, intuition, experimentation, and exploration, and I believe we want them to stay that way. But somehow, for most of us and for our children, those things fade into the background as the years pass. School and life become hard, filled with drudgery, repetition, and "have-to's." Joy, curiosity, wonder, intuition, experimentation, and exploration are shunted aside as the educational process moves forward. We are told that that is the way the process is meant to work: Our children must leave behind childish things like play, performance, invention, and wonder and redirect their attention toward organization, detail, and conformity to archaic concepts of work and the workplace. This is a pronouncement that comes from deep in our culture's past, from a historically distant moment that did not appreciate the boundless potential that all our children represent and did not understand that schools exist not to perpetuate the social order but to challenge and improve it.

In writing about Sarah's child, I want to contest those beliefs. I want to return to the children in this book and their words, drawings, and actions. Sophia, Donaldo, Tommy, Sabrina, Lucas, George, Susan, Bobbi, and the rest of my students have provided ample evidence of the richness of imagination as a resource for learning. I also want to return to myself as their teacher: It has been 10 years since Denzel presented me with the conundrum of imagination and sent me on this journey. My involvement with imagination, both my own and that of my students, has changed the way I view my world and my future. I see that I, like my students, am full with the potential of imagination. Imagination is a capacity of mind that we can all reclaim; it is never completely lost to us. We need a new paradigm for education that places imagination in the center of the process, and that paradigm is limited only by the imaginations of those who care about our children and the children themselves.

For teachers, living and working with imagination will alter how we teach but will not result in identical teaching practices. For our students and our children, the climate created in schools where imagination is at the center will affirm who they are as individuals, while also enabling them to recognize, identify, and form alliances with those who are different. But above all, reclaiming imagination will produce classrooms filled with joy and opportunity: multivocal, multimodal classrooms where literacy learning begins in the the body, with aspiration and the desire to know because the discourse we seek has become a necessity and the community we are a part of is creating a new and better vision of the world.

References

Anzaldua, G. (1987). *Borderlands: La frontera.* San Francisco: Spinsters/Aunt Lute Book Co.

Ashton-Warner, S. (1963). *Teacher.* New York: Simon & Schuster.

Babbit, N. (1969). *The search for delicious.* New York: Farrar, Strauss & Giroux.

Bachelard, G. (1971). *On poetic imagination and reverie.* New York: Bobbs-Merrill.

Bakhtin, M. (1981). *Discourse in the novel.* Austin: University of Texas Press.

Bakhtin, M. (1984). *Problems of Dostoevsky's poetics.* (C. Emerson, Ed. & Trans.) Minneapolis: University of Minnesota Press.

Bakhtin, M. M. (1986). *Speech genres and other late essays.* Austin: University of Texas Press.

Bakhtin, M. M. (1993). *Toward a philosophy of the act.* Austin: University of Texas Press.

Ballenger, C. (2003, April 26). "I would sing everyday": Imagination and skepticism. Keynote address, International Conference on Teacher Research, Lincolnshire, IL.

Ballenger, C. (1999). *Teaching other people's children.* New York: Teachers College Press.

Bauman, R. (1977). *Verbal art as performance.* Prospect Heights, IL: Waveland.

Brann, E. T. H. (1991). *The world of the imagination: Sum and substance.* Savage, MD: Rowman & Littlefield.

Brenner, B., & Bolognese, D. (1993). *Wagon wheels.* New York: HarperCollins.

Brookline Teacher Research Seminar. (2003). *Regarding children's talk: Teacher research on language and literacy.* New York: Teachers College Press.

Bruner, J. (1986). *Actual minds, possible worlds.* Cambridge, MA: Harvard University Press.

Cadwell, L. B. (1997). *Bringing Reggio Emilia home: An innovative approach to early childhood education.* New York: Teachers College Press.

Carini, P. (2001). *Starting strong: A different look at children, schools, and standards.* New York: Teachers College Press.

Cazden, C. (2001). *Classroom discourse: The language of teaching and learning.* Portsmouth, NH: Heinemann.

Clifton, L. (1992) *The boy who didn't believe in spring.* New York: Dutton.

Cobb, E. (1993). *The ecology of imagination in childhood.* Austin, TX: Spring.

Cochran-Smith, M. (1984). *The making of a reader.* Norwood, NJ: Ablex.

Coleridge, S. T. (1907). *Biographia literaria.* London: Oxford University Press.

Corbin, H. (1969). *Creative imagination in the Sufism of Ibn Arabi.* Princeton, NJ: Princeton University Press.

Dalghiesh, A. (1991). *The courage of Sarah Noble.* New York: Simon & Schuster.

DeBono, E. (1969). *The mechanism of mind.* New York: Simon & Schuster.

DeBono, E. (1970). *Lateral thinking: A textbook of creativity.* London: Ward Lock Educational.

de Chardin, T. (1960). *The divine milieu.* New York: Harper & Brothers.

Dennison, G. (1969). *The lives of children: The story of the First Street School.* New York: Random House.

Donaldson, M. (1963). *A study of children's thinking.* New York: Norton.

Dyson, A. (1993). *Social worlds of children learning to write in an urban primary school.* New York: Teachers College Press.

Dyson, A. (1999). Coach Bombay's kids learn to write: Children's appropriation of media material for school literacy. *Research in the Teaching of English, 33,* 367–402.

Edwards, C., Gandini, L., & Forman, G. (1993). *The hundred languages of children: The Reggio Emilia approach to early childhood education.* Norwood, NJ: Ablex.

Edwards, D., & Mercer, N. (1987). *Common knowledge: The development of understanding in the classroom.* London: Methuen.

Eisner, E. (1976). *The arts, human development and education.* Berkeley, CA: McCutchan.

Emerson, R. W. (1983) *Nature; addresses and lectures.* Reprinted in J. Porte (Ed.), *Emerson: Essays and lectures.* New York: The Library of America. (Original work published 1849)

Estrada, K., & McClaren, P. (1993). A dialogue on multiculturalism and democratic culture. *Educational Researcher, 22*(3), 27–33.

Fleck, L. (1979). *Genesis and development of a scientific fact.* Chicago: University of Chicago Press.

Forbes, E. (1943). *Johnny Tremain.* New York: Houghton-Mifflin.

Fox-Keller, E. (1983). *A feeling for the organism: The life and work of Barbara McClintock.* New York: Freeman.

Friere, P. (1972). *Pedagogy of the oppressed.* London: Penguin.

Freire, P., & Macedo, D. (1987). *Literacy: Reading the word and the world.* New York: Bergin & Garvey.

Frye, N. (1964). *The educated imagination.* Bloomington: University of Indiana Press.

Gallas, K. (1994). *The languages of learning: How children talk, write, dance, draw, and sing their understanding of the world.* New York: Teachers College Press.

Gallas, K. (1995). *Talking their way into science: Hearing children's questions and theories, responding with curricula.* New York: Teachers College Press.

Gallas, K. (1998). *"Sometimes I can be anything": Power, gender and identity in a primary classroom.* New York: Teachers College Press.

Gallas, K., & Smagorinsky, P. (2001). Approaching texts in school. *The Reading Teacher, 56*(1), 54–67.

Gardner, H. (1973). *The arts and human development.* New York: Wiley.

Gardner, H. (1980). *Artful scribbles.* New York: Basic Books.

Gardner, H. (1982). *Art, mind, & brain: A cognitive approach to creativity.* New York: Basic Books.

Gee, J. P. (1996). *Social linguistics and literacies: Ideology in discourses.* London: Falmer.

Goelman, H., Oberg, A., & Smith, F. (Eds.). (1984). *Awakening to literacy.* Exeter, NH: Heinemann.

Graham, K. (1980). *Wind in the willows.* New York: Holt.

Greene, M. (1995). *Releasing the imagination: Essays on education, the arts, and social change.* New York: Jossey-Bass.

Grotowski, J. (1968). *Towards a poor theater.* New York: Simon & Schuster.

Grumet, M. (1988). *Bitter milk.* Amherst: University of Massachusetts Press.

Halliday, M. A. K. (1975). *Learning how to mean: Exploration in the development of language.* New York: Elsevier North-Holland.

Heath, S. B. (1982). What no bedtime story means: Narrative skills at home and school. *Language in Society, 11,* 49–76.

Heath, S. B. (1983). *Ways with words: Language, life, and work in communities and classrooms.* New York: Cambridge University Press.

Heath, S. B. (1986). Separating "things of the imagination" from life: Learning to read and write. In W. H. Teale & E. Sulzby (Eds.), *Emergent literacy: Writing and reading* (pp. 156–172). Norwood, NJ: Ablex.

Heath, S. B., & Thomas, C. (1984). The achievement of preschool literacy for mother and child. In H. Goelman, A. Oberg, & F. Smith (Eds.), *Awakening to literacy* (pp. 51–72). Exeter, NH: Heinemann.

Holton, G. (1973). *Thematic origins of scientific thought.* Cambridge, MA: Harvard University Press.

Holton, G. (1978). *The scientific imagination: Case studies.* New York: Cambridge University Press.

Hull, G., & Schultz, K. (2001). Literacy and learning out of school: A review of theory and research. *Review of Educational Research 71*(4), 575–611.

John-Steiner, V. (1985). *Notebooks of the mind: Explorations of thinking.* New York: Harper & Row.

John-Steiner, V. (2000). *Creative collaboration.* New York: Oxford University Press.

John-Steiner, V., & Meehan, T. (1999). Creativity and collaboration in knowledge construction. In C. D. Lee & P. Smagorinsky (Eds.), *Vygotskian perspectives on literacy research: Constructing meaning through collaborative inquiry.* New York: Cambridge University Press.

Kant, I. (1969). *Critique of pure reason.* New York: Dutton. (Original work published 1786)

Kearney, R. (1998). *The wake of imagination: Towards a postmodern culture.* London: Routledge.

Kellogg, R. (1967). *The psychology of children's art.* New York: Random House.

Kroll, S. (1984). *The biggest pumpkin ever.* New York: Holiday House.

Lave, J., & Wenger, E. (1991). *Situated learning: Legitimate peripheral participation.* New York: Cambridge University Press.

Lemke, J. (1990). *Talking science: Language, learning and values.* Norwood, NJ: Ablex.

Lenski, L. (1995). *Indian captive: The story of Mary Jemison.* New York: Harper-Trophy.

Lensmire, T. J. (1994). Writing workshops as carnival: Reflections on an alternative learning environment. *Harvard Educational Review, 64,* 371–391.

Lensmire, T. J. (1997). The teacher as Dostoevskian novelist. *Research in the Teaching of English, 31,* 367–392.

Lessing, D. (1994). *Under my skin: Volume one of my autobiography, to 1949.* New York: HarperCollins.

Lewis, C. S. (1956). *Surprised by joy: The shaping of my early life.* New York: Harcourt Brace.

Medawar, P. (1982). *Pluto's republic.* Oxford: Oxford University Press.

Mehan, H. (1979). *Learning lessons: Social organization in the classroom.* Cambridge, MA: Harvard University Press.

Moeri, L. (1981). *Save Queen of Sheba.* New York: Dutton.

Moll, L. (1992). Bilingual classroom studies and community readings: Some recent trends. *Educational Researcher, 21*(3), 20–24.

Morson, G. S., & Emerson, C. (1990). *Mikhail Bakhtin: Creation of a prosaics.* Stanford, CA: Stanford University Press.

Nabokov, V. (1967). *Speak memory.* New York: Vintage.

Nash, P. (1966). *Authority and freedom in education: An introduction to the philosophy of education.* New York: Wiley.

Nemerov, H. (1978). *Figures of thought.* Boston: Godine.

New London Group. (1996). A pedagogy of multiliteracies: Designing social futures. *Harvard Educational Review, 66*(1), 60–92.

Nicol, A. (1990). *Maroo of the winter caves.* New York: Clarion.

Ninio, A., & Bruner, J. S. (1976). The achievement and antecedents of labeling. *Journal of Child Language, 5,* 1–15.

Noddings, N. (1992). *The challenge to care in schools: An alternative approach to education.* New York: Teachers College Press.

Ochs, E., Jacoby, S., & Gonzales, P. (1996). "When I come down I'm in the domain state": Grammar and graphic representation in the interpretive activity of physicists. In E. Ochs, E. S. Schegloff, & S. A. Thompson (Eds.), *Interaction and grammar* (pp. 328–369). New York: Cambridge University Press.

O'Dell, S. (1970). *Sing down the moon.* Boston: Houghton Mifflin.

Paley, V. G. (1990). *The boy who would be a helicopter.* Cambridge, MA: Harvard University Press.

Paley, V. G. (1993). *You can't say you can't play.* Cambridge, MA: Harvard University Press.

Paton, J. W. (1982). *The green book.* New York: Farrar, Strauss & Giroux.

Paulsen, G. (2000). *Hatchet.* New York: Simon & Schuster.

Paz, O. (1990). *The other voice: Essays on modern poetry.* New York: Harcourt Brace Jovanovich.

Raymo, C. (1987). *Honey from stone: A naturalist's search for God.* St. Paul: Hungry Mind Press.

Richardson, E. (1964). *In the early world.* New York: Pantheon.

Root-Bernstein, R. S. (1989). *Discovering: Inventing and solving problems at the frontier of scientific knowledge.* Cambridge, MA: Harvard University Press.

Rosenblatt, L. (1978). *The reader, the text, the poem: The transactional theory of literary work.* Carbondale: Southern Illinois University Press.

Rothenberg, A. (1979). *The emerging goddess: The creative process in art, science, and other fields.* Chicago: University of Chicago Press.

Salk, J. (1983). *The anatomy of reality.* New York: Columbia University Press.

Sartre, J. P. (1961). *The psychology of imagination.* New York: Citadel.

Sartre, J. P. (1964). *The words.* Greenwich, CT: Fawcett.

Schwartz, E. G. (1995). Crossing borders/shifting paradigms: Multiculturalism and children's literature. *Harvard Educational Review, 65*(4), 634–650.

Scollon, R., & Scollon, B. K. (1981). *Narrative, literacy and face in inter-ethnic communication.* Norwood, NJ: Ablex.

Scribner, S., & Cole, M. (1981). *The psychology of literacy.* Cambridge, MA: Harvard University Press.

Silverstein, S. (1981). *A light in the attic.* New York: Harper & Row.

Slattery, D. P. (2002, December). *Underworld knowing is mythic knowing.* Public lecture. Pacifica Graduate Institute, Carpenteria, CA.

Smagorinsky, P. (2001). If reading is constructed, what's it made from? Toward a cultural theory of reading. *Review of Educational Research, 71,* 133–169.

Smagorinsky, P., & Coppock, J. (1994). Cultural tools and the classroom context. *Written Communication, 11,* 283–310.

Speare, E. G. (1983). *Sign of the beaver.* Boston: Houghton Mifflin.

Steig, W. (1986a). *Abel's island.* New York: Farrar, Straus & Giroux.

Steig, W. (1986b). *Brave Irene.* New York: Farrar, Straus & Giroux.

Steig, W. (1987). *Sylvester and the magic pebble.* New York: Aladdin Library.

Sterling, O. (1954). *Freedom train.* New York: Scholastic.

Stevens, W. (1960). *The necessary angel: Essays on reality and the imagination.* London: Faber & Faber.

Street, B. V. (1993). The new literacy studies: Guest editorial. *Journal of Research in Reading, 16*(2), 81–97.

Street, B. V. (1995). *Social literacies: Critical approaches to literacy in development, ethnography and education.* London: Longman.

Swaim, J. (1998). In search of an honest response. *Language Arts, 75,* 118–125.

Swaim, J. (2002). Laughing together in carnival: A tale of two writers. *Language Arts, 79,* 337–346.

Taylor, D. (1983). *Family literacy: Young children learning to read and write.* Portsmouth, NH: Heinemann.

Teale, W. H. (1986). Home background and young children's literacy development. In W. H. Teale & E. Sulzby (Eds.), *Emergent literacy: Writing and reading* (pp. 173–204). Norwood, NJ: Ablex.

Turner, A. (1989). *Grasshopper summer.* New York: Simon & Schuster.

Warnock, M. (1976). *Imagination.* Berkeley: University of California Press.

Warren, B., Ballenger, C., Ogonowski, M., Rosebery, A., & Hudicourt-Barnes, J. (2000). *Re-thinking diversity in learning science: The logic of everyday languages.* Cambridge, MA: TERC, Cheche Konnen Center.

Wertsch, J. V. (1991). *Voices of the mind: A sociocultural approach to mediated action.* Cambridge, MA: Harvard University Press.

Wolf, S. A., & Heath, S. B. (1992). *The braid of literature: Children's worlds of reading.* Cambridge, MA: Harvard University Press.

Wolpert, L., & Richards, A. (1997). *Passionate minds: The inner world of scientists.* Oxford: Oxford University Press.

Wood, A., & Wood, D. (1987). *Heckedy Peg.* New York: Harcourt Brace.

Index

Italic letter *f* following a page number refers to a figure.

About the Author

Karen Gallas is an early childhood and elementary teacher with more than 30 years of experience in urban and rural public schools. She received her doctorate in education from Boston University in 1981. Her work as a teacher-researcher began in the Brookline Teacher Research Seminar. It has focused on the role of the arts in teaching and learning, on children's language in the classroom, and on the process of teacher research. She has published three books, *The Languages of Learning: How Children Talk, Write, Dance, Draw and Sing Their Understanding of the World* (1994); *Talking Their Way into Science: Hearing Children's Questions and Theories, Responding with Curriculum* (1995); and *"Sometimes I Can Be Anything": Power, Gender and Identity in a Primary Classroom* (1998).